THE CATHOLIC UNIVERSITY OF AMERICA
STUDIES IN CANON AND ROMAN LAW

VOL. 41

CHURCH PROPERTY: MODES OF ACQUISITION

A DISSERTATION

Submitted to the Faculty of Canon Law of the Catholic University of America in partial fulfilment of the requirements for the Degree of

DOCTOR OF CANON AND ROMAN LAW

BY

WILLIAM J. DOHENY, C.S.C., A.B., J.U.L.

Nihil Obstat:
✠ THOMAS JOSEPH SHAHAN, S.T.D., Censor Deputatus.

Imprimatur:
✠ MICHAEL J. CURLEY, D.D., Archiepiscopus Baltimorensis.

Imprimi potest:
GEORGE J. FINNIGAN, C.S.C., Provincialis.

FOREWORD.

There is hardly any subject more intimately bound up with the history and development of the Church than that of its temporalities. The history of its means and methods of acquiring property presents to the student of jurisprudence the story of its vicissitudes and its triumphs. In many instances its decretal collections and conciliar enactments may be verily devoid of the romantic interest and the picturesque grouping that constitute the charm of other topics of its history, but a deeper knowledge of the Church's legislation on the modes of acquisition of property throughout the centuries cannot but make for a clearer understanding and appreciation of the rulings of the Code on this matter.

In this country the question of the acquisition of Church property has been important and at the same time perplexing. It has engaged the attention of our most prominent churchmen for the past century and has been discussed in practically every synod or council. The ten provincial as well as the three plenary councils of Baltimore were constrained to deal with the subject. In 1829 the Bishops assembled at the First Provincial Council of Baltimore invited Mr. R. B. Taney, afterwards Chief Justice of the Supreme Court, to advise them on points of American law concerning property rights. From that time the matter has remained one of great practical concern for all the members of the Church.

No section of the Code, perhaps, contains more marked a departure from the former legislation than does Title XXVII of Book III, the matter under consideration in the present monograph. A considerable amount of the previous legislation is changed but the most noteworthy innovation brought about by the Code is that of Canons 1508 and 1513 § 2 whereby Civil Law is canonized as providing norms of procedure in most matters concerning prescription and last wills. This significant change can unreservedly be called epoch-making. It indicates a closer approximation to the harmony and mutual helpfulness of the

Middle Ages between the ecclesiastical and civil systems of law. It bespeaks, as a harbinger of a bright future, the return of concord and understanding between the two powers as outlined so ingeniously by Pope Boniface VIII in his celebrated constitution, "Unam sanctam."[1]

In this brief study of the modes of acquisition of ecclesiastical property the aim has been to discuss and open new vistas of thought, to suggest and stimulate interest rather than to attempt to say the last word on each point. Such an effort were sheer folly where laws, like other human institutions, evolve and develop not by measurable marches on a stable course, but under varying influences difficult of discernment. The most that any study can do is to strive to ascertain the courses of events and to discover the different factors influencing past legislation in order to understand the present and to pave the way for the formulation of laws of development for the future.

In the compilation of the footnotes of this study, the aim has been to make the references to sources and authors suggestive rather than exhaustive. It has not been the intention of the writer to frame a long categorical list of citations to corroborate each statement, for this method seems futile in sciences like Canon Law and Theology where scores of similar opinions must of necessity be repeated by many authors. The aim has been rather to trace the paternity of new ideas to the originators. Sometimes, however, more copious references are subjoined either to confirm assertions in the text or to direct the readers to sources of fuller information.

This dissertation is one of a series of monographs on Church Property under the direction of the School of Canon Law of the University. The first, *The Tenure of Parochial Property in the United States of America,* was published in 1926 by Reverend Doctor C. J. Bartlett. A study on *Canonical Juristic Personality* is being published this year by Mr. Brendan Brown, J. U. D. The aim of the School of Canon Law is to complete the series within a few years with dissertations on the administration and alienation of Church Property.

The writer terminates this work with a sincere expression of gratitude to his professors: Reverend Doctor H. L. Motry, Reverend Doctor V. T. Schaaf, O. F. M., Reverend Doctor F.

[1]C. 1, de maioritate et obedientia I, 8 in Extravag. com.

Lardone and Doctor Manoel de Oliveira Lima, for the kind direction and generous assistance received throughout his course. In particular is he grateful to the Right Reverend Monsignor Filippo Bernardini, S.T.D., J.U.D., whose inspirational scholarship and kindly friendship he has appreciated. He likewise takes pleasure in acknowledging his indebtedness to the Reverend Doctor M. A. Mathis, C.S.C., for generous encouragement and untold kindness.

TABLE OF CONTENTS.

CHAPTER I.

Historical Concept.

THE Church in declaring its right in Canon 1495 to acquire, possess and administer temporal goods for the attainment of its own end is but restating a doctrine that has been held from the beginning of Christianity.[1] It received this right from its Divine Founder and has steadfastly vindicated it throughout the centuries against heretics as well as unjust aggressors.[2] Intended and instituted as a perfect and independent society the Church derives this right from its very nature and its work.[3] Its object, as defined by Christ, is to lead men to salvation and it has the right to employ means that tend directly or indirectly toward that end.[4]

From the nature of its work among men it is necessary that the Church foster forms of worship consonant with the nature of its members who are not disembodied spirits, but beings composed of body and soul.[5] The doctrine of the Church, then, must be clothed in forms that satisfy men's hearts and must be vivified with external manifestations of men's inner feelings. In a word

---

[1] *Didache*, XII, 3; Funk, *Doctrina Duodecim Apostolorum*, 41. *Constitutiones Sanctorum Apostolorum*, VII; Funk, 95. *Codex Theodosianus*, 16, 1, 4; 16, 2, 16; 16, 2, 26; 16, 2, 36. C. Ancyranum (314), can. 15, *Ss. Conc.* II, 518. C. Antiochen (341), can. 24, *Ss. Conc.* II, 1327. C. Chalcedonensis (451), can. 2, Actionisi VI, *Ss. Conc.* VII, 175. C. Toletanum (633), can. 33, *Ss. Conc.* X, 628.

[2] St. Augustinus, *In Evang. Joann.*, Tract. LXII, 5, M.P.L. XXXV, 1805. C. 13, *de electione et elect. potestate*, I, 5 in VI°. C. 1, *de immunitate ecclesiarum, coemeteriorum et aliorum locorum relig.*, III, 23, in VI.° Joannes XXII, Const., *Licet inter doctrinam*, 23 Oct. 1323, Denz.-Bann. 494–500. Joannes XXII, Const. *Cum inter nonnullos*, 13 Nov. 1323, Denz.-Bann., 494–500. Joannes XXII, Const. *Licet*, 23 Oct. 1327, *Fontes*, n. 38. Martinus V, Const. *Inter cunctas*, 22 Feb. 1418, *Fontes* n. 43.

[3] Leo XIII, ep. encycl., *Immortale Dei*, 1 Nov. 1885, *Fontes*, n. 592. Tarquini, *Iuris Eccles. Publici Institutiones*, 31.

[4] Palmieri, *Tractatus de Romano Pontifice*, 119. Mazzella, *De religione et ecclesia*, 442.

[5] III Conc. Plen. Baltimor. n. 264. Conc. Plen. Americae Latinae n. 824. Vogt, *Das Kirchliche Vermögensrecht*, 5. *Principles of Almsdeeds*, *Eccles. Review*, XXXVI (1907), 137.

the senses as well as the souls of human beings must be reckoned with and captivated. Hence external and visible means are employed by the Church, as Christ intended, to foster and aid the expression of internal religious sentiments. The ministration of the sacraments, religious worship and ceremonies postulate the existence of churches, altars, vestments and the like. The Church needs temples: that sacrifice be offered to God in fitting places; that the faithful—to the edification of one another—might congregate for prayer, the reception of the sacraments and the hearing of the word of God. For the reverent performance of the liturgy sacred vessels, altars and vestments are required together with the other necessary or ornamental adjuncts of sacrifice. All this indicates the validity of the Church's right to acquire whatever is necessary for the attainment of its purpose.

Since the Church is a public society with public functions and forms of worship it has need of ministers to perform the sacred rites and to act as mediators between the Creator and the creature. That these are entitled to support is amply evidenced in Scripture for as St. Paul says:—"The Lord ordained that they who preach the gospel should live by the gospel;"[1] "I have taken from other churches, receiving wages of them for your ministry."[2] Moreover, the Church needs temporalities to support and protect the poor, the sick and the unsheltered who as God's chosen ones are the Church's truest treasures.[3] Since the Church is subject to temporal needs and exigencies just like other independent and perfect societies, temporal goods not only become useful but are lawful and necessary for the continuance of the work of Christ on earth.[4]

The validity and necessity of the Church's right of acquisition are borne out by the constant practice since Apostolic and patristic times;[5] by numerous and uniform declarations of the

---

[1] I Cor. IX: 14.

[2] II Cor. XI: 8.

[3] St. Justinus, *Apologia*, I, 67, MPG, VI, 430. C. Bracarense II (563), cap. VII, *Ss. Conc.* IX, 778. P. Fourneret, *Biens Ecclesiastiques*, *Dict. de Theol. Cath.*, II, 1, col. 854.

[4] III Conc. Plen. Baltimor. n. 264. Pruemmer, 518. Scheys, 90.

[5] St. Paul, I. Cor. IX:14. St. Cyprianus, *De unitate Ecclesiae*, c. 26; MPL, IV, 535; *Epistola LXVI*, MPL, IV, 410. Tertullianus, *Apologia*, c. 39, MPL, I, 532. St. Augustinus, *Sermo* CCLXXVII, MPL, XXXIX, 2266. St. Hieronymus, *In Ezechialem* XLVI, MPL, XXV, 457; *in Malachiam* III, 7 MPL, XXV, 1569.

Church;[1] by the teachings of the theologians as well as by the consensus of opinion of Christian peoples.

While instructing His disciples in the way of the spiritual life, Christ never stigmatized the right of acquiring property nor did He fail to guide His followers in the use and administration of all the temporal goods that came to them. He saw that the ministers of His Gospel could not depend for support solely on the generous whims of the populace. He accordingly appointed Judas in charge of the purse from which the needs of the little band were supplied;[2] and St. Peter was commissioned to pay the tributes.[3] Commenting on this St. Augustine succinctly expounds the teaching of Christ and the Church:—"The Lord, therefore, had also a money-box, where He kept the offerings of believers and distributed to the necessities of His own, and to others who were in need. It was then that the custom of having church-money was first introduced, so that thereby we might understand that His precept about taking no thought for the morrow was not a command that no money should be kept by His saints, but that God should not be served for any such end, and that the doing of what is right should not be held in abeyance through fear of want."[4]

In acquiring temporalities the Apostles but followed the example of their Master. The infant Church needed resources to carry on its work. It accordingly appealed to the faithful to make offerings at the sacrifice of the Mass, to give of their surplus goods for the alleviation of poverty and to be generous in their support of God's ministers who "ministering in the holy places" had a right to "eat the things that are of the holy place and partake with the altar."[5]

---

[1] Joannes XXII, const., *Cum inter nonnullos*, 13 Nov. 1323, Denz.-Bann. n. 494–500. Joannes XXII, const. *Licet*, 23 Oct. 1327, *Fontes* n. 38. Martinus V, const., *Inter cunctas*, 22 Feb. 1418, *Fontes*, 43. Clemens XIII, const., *Alias ad Apostolatus*, 30 Jan. 1768, *Fontes* n. 464. Pius IX, allocut. *Quibus luctuosissimis*, 5 Sept. 1851, *Fontes* n. 512.

[2] St. John, XII:6;XIII:29.

[3] St. Matthew, XVII:26.

[4] St. Augustinus, *In Evang. Joann.* Tract. LXII, n. 5, MPL, XXXV, 1805. St. Augustine, *Nicene and Post-Nicene Fathers* (First Series) VII, 314. Ven. Beda, *In Lucae Evang. Expositio*, Lib. IV, Cap. XII, MPL, XCII, 494.

[5] I Cor. IX:13.

1. Acquisition of Temporal Goods Prior to the Edict of Milan.

During the first three centuries the principal means whereby the Church acquired property were:—Mass offerings, tributes and largesses. These were considered the most reliable means to support the various activities and the extensive charities of the Church. The faithful realized the sacredness of the Sacrifice instituted by Christ and gave generously of their goods at the Mass. These offerings were made at the Offertory and usually were contributions of bread, incense, oil, grapes and wine.[1] The bread and wine were employed in the Eucharistic Sacrifice while the rest was distributed to the clergy and the poor.[2] Offerings of this nature were proffered every time the faithful attended Mass in acknowledgment of God's supreme dominion and in thanksgiving for His countless benisons. To the early Christians these offerings signified union with God and participation in the Divine Sacrifice. Hence the entire congregation of worshippers brought gifts so that the oblation of their goods might be blessed together with the oblation of their hearts. As the custom of attending Mass daily was general in the first centuries the amount of such gifts was unquestionably very great, at least in the larger communities.[3] That such contributions signified communion with God and His Church is clear from the fact that they could not be accepted indiscriminately from everyone. Thus the offerings of public sinners, suicides and oppressors of the poor were repudiated.[4]

With the progress of centuries many worshippers found it inconvenient to bring offerings to the Sacrifice of the Mass, while others became remiss in their duty. It was then that the custom

---

[1] Benedictus XIV, *De Synodo Dioecesana*, V. 8. Thomassinus, III, 1, 12, n. 1. Rätzinger, *Geschicte der Kirchlichen Armenpflege*, 112. The ceremony of presenting candles, bread, wine, water, two turtle doves, two pigeons and smaller birds is still preserved in the Mass of canonization of saints. T. F. Macken, *The Canonization of Saints*, Dublin, (1910), 255.

[2] Thomassinus, III, 1, 4, n, 2; II, 12, 1–5; III, 26, 1-10.

[3] *Constitutiones Apostolici*, VII, 12, 19; Funk, 83, 95. St. Justinus, *Apologia*, LXVII, 8, MPG, VI, 430. Tertullianus, *Apologia*, c. 39, MPL, I, 532. Ratzinger, 113. Uhlhorn, 144.

[4] C. Carthaginense IV (398), can. 93, 94, *Ss. Conc.* III, 958. St. J. Chrysostomus, *Homilia* XXVII *in I. Cor.* XI, 17, MPG, LXI, 227. St. J. Chrysostomus, *Homilia XXXI in Matt.* IV, MPG, LVII, 369. Tertullianus, *De praescriptione haereticorum*, 20, MPL, II, 49. Schmalzgrueber, III, 3, 30, n. 92. Thomassinus, III, 1, 12.

of substituting money came into vogue with the consequent institution of the system of Mass stipends, in order that the ministerial fruits of the Sacrifice might be applied more equitably.[1]

Under the classification of tributes were included the fees and offerings not made in direct relation to the Mass. These were intended principally for the support of the clergy and the maintenance of ecclesiastical institutions, but they were extended to the needy of the laity whenever the occasion demanded. During the first centuries these offerings were purely voluntary, as Tertullian avers: "We have a treasure chest; it is not made of purchase-money as a religion that has its price. On the monthly day, if he likes, each puts in a small donation; but only if it be his pleasure and only if he be able: for there is no compulsion; all is voluntary."[2] At a later date, however, the universality of the custom of giving engendered an obligation to which all the faithful were bound. When they forgot this custom they were rebuked as having failed in a serious duty.[3] The shepherds of Christ's flock knew that offerings were means of bringing the faithful into closer union with one another and of giving them a clearer understanding of the value of the Mass and their religion. They likewise understood Christ's intention of building His religion on sacrifice. They saw—with their shrewd knowledge of human nature—that people are interested in whatever entails sacrifice for them, and when they cease to make the sacrifice their interest lapses and their religious feelings wither. Now the usual sacrifice that the ordinary individual made in the earlier centuries—as even in our own day—was to give of the money and temporal goods he so dearly loved for the continuance of Christ's work and the maintenance of Christ's ministers on earth.

Largesses included the more generous donations made by the rich as an acknowledgment of God's goodness to them. Thus Pammachius, a member of the Senate and descendant of Roman consuls converted his home and estate into a church and hostel for the poor.[4] Similar gifts of property and buildings were made

[1] Benedictus XIV, *De Synodo Dioecesana,* V, 8, n. 1. Devoti, XVI, 540. Lugo, *De sanctissima Eucharistia,* disp. 21, n. 1. Gasparri, *De Sanctissima Eucharistia,* I, 535.

[2] Tertullian, *Apology,* c. 39, *Ante-Nicene Fathers,* III, 46.

[3] St. Cyprianus, *De opere et eleemosynis,* c. 26, MPL, IV, 643. St. Augustinus, *In Psalm. CXLVI, n.* 17, MPL, XXXVII, 1911. Origen, *Homilia XI in Numeros,* MPG. XII, 644.

[4] St. Hieronymus, *Epistola* LXVI, n. 6, MPL, XXII, 641. Paulinus Nolanis, *Epistola* XIII *ad Pammachium,* 15, MPL, LXI, 216, 555.

by St. Marcella, Paula, Eustochium,[1] Fabiola, Lea, Oceanus, Domnio, Pinianus, by members of the Valerian, Anician, Acilian and Uranian families.[2] The early Christians considered the superfluities of the rich to be the necessities of the poor,[3] so that the gifts of the wealthy were looked upon as a sort of voluntary and generous restitution to the needy. All this was but in conformity with the Christian idea of temporal possessions which is that of stewardship whereby the service of God and the good of one's neighbor may be advanced and for which a strict accounting must be rendered on the day of judgment.

The early Church did not scruple about acquiring vast amounts of temporalities for it used them conscientiously for the alleviation of poverty and suffering.[4] Before the Christian era the condition of the poor and incapacitated was much more abject than is their state now. Charity, as understood today, was practically unknown in the pagan world of antiquity. Compassion was no Hellenic virtue and still less was it a Roman trait. The needs of the indigent and helpless passed unnoticed with no claim to assistance from individuals or society.[5] No benevolent organizations interested themselves in social welfare or philanthropic work. The intellectual and philosophical achievements of the Greeks had not brought into being a full grasp of the bond of common philanthropy; nor had the marvellous legal system of the Romans conceived of principles of universal equality and charity.

The Church entered a world cold and uncharitable toward the helpless and immediately assumed the role of dispenser of earthly as well as heavenly gifts. It acquired freely; freely did it give. Thus St. Paul repeatedly expressed his solicitude for the poor and even collected funds to relieve their straitened conditions.[6] The special office of deaconship was instituted to aid the Apostles to carry on their charitable work more extensively.

As the Church's acquisitions increased its charity expanded. Wherever it went it held out a helping hand to the poor, the

---

[1] *Epistola Paulae et Eustochii ad Marcellam XLVI*, MPL, XXII, 490.

[2] Grisar, *History of Rome and the Popes*, I, 59.

[3] St. Augustinus, *In Evang. Matt.*, Sermo LXI, c. 11, MPL, XXXVIII, 411.

[4] Tertullian, *De fuga in persecutione*, XII, MPL, II, 135. St. Justinus, *Apologia*, I, n. 67, MPG, VI, 430.

[5] Kirby, *Social Mission of Charity*, 116. Uhlhorn, 3, 15, 60. Bogardus, *A History of Social Thought*, (Los Angeles), (1922), 123–128.

[6] Roman. XV:26; Acts XI:29;I Cor. XVI:1–3.

enslaved and the unfortunate.[1] Each Christian community did all in its power to support its indigent; and aimed moreover to aid the younger and poorer communities by benefactions.[2] This all-embracing charity was the distinguishing trait that impressed the pagans with the sublimity of Christ's teaching.[3] It was the soul that gave harmony and cohesion to the body of the faithful, the animating principle of individual conduct and the guide of social relationship.[4] And no one was excluded from this charity of the Church. Widows, orphans, exiles, captives, prisoners, lepers, the sick, the plague-stricken, travellers, strangers and unbelievers were honored and helped as mortals destined for Christ's redeeming graces.[5] During the pontificate of Cornelius (251–252) fifteen hundred widows and poor people were supported by the Church at Rome.[6]

Such extensive charitable work and the actual possession of a vast amount of temporalities indicate that the Church acquired considerable property during the first centuries. That most of this property came from purely voluntary donations was due to the happy combination of various factors. The first fervor of the faithful was still burning with an ardent flame; almsgiving was spontaneous and abundant; Christianity meant a sacrifice that only strong, generous and sincere men could make; Christians were earnest with the earnestness of youth; heresies had not become persistent or powerful enough to infect the Christian polity with the virus of their errors.

Property acquired in the various ways indicated became the Church's own in the full sense of the term of ownership. The Church was not considered merely as an authoritative administrator acting as an agent for donors. Whatever was acquired, either by tribute or voluntary donation became the veritable property of the Church. It was with this understanding that the

---

[1] Tertullianus, *Apologia*, c. 39, MPL, I, 532.

[2] Eusebius, *Historia Ecclesiae*, IV, 23, MPG, XX, 367.

[3] Tertullianus, *Apologia*, c. 39, MPL, I, 471. St. Ignatius, *Epistola ad Romanos*, MPG, V, 802.

[4] Uhlhorn 158. Sohm, *Kirchenrecht*, 71.

[5] *Constitutiones Apostolicae* IV, 8; MPG, I, 819; V, 1, MPG, I, 830. St. Coelestinus Papa, *Epistola XXIII ad Theodosium*, MPL, L. 546. Tertullianus, *Apologia*, c. 39, MPL, I, 532. St. Justinus, *Apologia*, I, n. 67, MPG, VI, 430. St. Cyprianus, *Epistola 36*, MPL, IV, 327. St. Hieronymus, *Epistola LXVI*, n. 55, MPL, XXII, 641. Paulinus Nolanus, *Epistola XIII ad Pammachium*, n. 15, MPL, LXI, 216.

[6] Eusebius, *Historia Ecclesiae*, VI, 43. MPG, XX, 622.

early Christians and the faithful of succeeding centuries gave to the Church. Gifts and donations constituted outright transfers of ownership and the Church was free to use its temporalities as it saw fit provided the pious intentions of donors were carried out.

The first three centuries can be considered the formative period in which customs of property acquisition, charity and church-support shaped themselves. In the first communities of faithful at Jerusalem, Antioch and Rome there was no pre-ordained system of acquiring temporalities. Collections were taken up when the occasion demanded; landed property was frequently turned into personal and offered to the common fund by souls of heroic virtue; and generally the individual Christians gave the amounts that their own personal generosity suggested. Gradually, however, a definite system was being elaborated. It was necessary for the common good to regulate to some extent the amounts, the times, the methods of giving. Under the Old Law first-fruits and tithes had proved to be practicable means of support. Similar systems were easily adjusted to the needs of the Church. These were incorporated into the ordinances of the councils and sanctioned as a part of the organized and equitable system of Church support. With these systematized means of securing temporalities the Church was preparing itself for the great task of caring for the throngs of needy inhabitants of a disintegrating empire.[1]

2. From the Edict of Milan to the Council of Trent.

Toward the beginning of the fourth century the effects of the decadence of the Roman Empire began to be felt. The political hegemony of Rome was breaking down and upheavals became frequent in its social organization. Every social and political cataclysm threw thousands upon charity and these multitudes looked to the Church for help. Thus the system of community and congregational charity of the first three centuries changed almost of necessity into wholesale alms-giving and institutional organizations of relief. Previously only isolated cases had called forth the Church's tenderest ministrations of charity; but as the empire of Rome disintegrated wholesale pauperism of the most terrible kind sought relief from the Church. Increased demands on the Church's charity in turn necessitated changes in the lineaments of its system of securing temporal goods.

[1] Ratzinger 113. Uhlhorn 158.

No member of the Christian polity, knowing the merit of even the cup of cold water given in Christ's name,[1] could turn a deaf ear to constant pleas for help. The Church was the official spokesman pleading the cause of the needy. Its members responded generously. Consequently the Church was constantly acquiring more property and thus the sphere of its usefulness was ever extending. During this same period Constantine granted full property rights to the Church. Donations, legacies, estates, and valuable gifts were then acquired with reasonable assurance of security.[2]

In order to systematize and control the acquisition of church property at this time the bishops had to assume direct management of the means of acquiring property as well as of the property itself when acquired. This closer supervision was necessary to protect the faithful from impostors and church property from exploitation. The Councils likewise found it necessary to legislate about Church property. Their enactments made it clear that property was acquired for the Church's benefit and not the emolument of individual pastors and bishops; secondly that property once acquired was to be held as a sacred trust. Thus the Council of Ancyra insisted that property acquired by the Church could not be disposed of by priests without proper permission from the bishop.[3] The Council Antioch warned bishops to safeguard all temporalities acquired by the Church to avoid confusion at their death.[4] The Third Council of Arles forbade priests to jeopardize property acquired by the Church by entering into onerous contracts.[5] The Fourth Council of Toledo emphasized the sacredness of property acquired for the Church by forbidding bishops to take more than their allotted incomes from the Church funds.[6] According to a ruling of the Fifth Council of Arles the administrators of churches, monasteries and hospitals were forbidden to violate property acquired for the Church.[7] Since church goods were acquired by the Church and not the individual administrators, bishops were forbidden by the Second Council of Nice to donate or transfer such treasured

---

[1] St. Matthew X:42; St. Mark IX:40.

[2] *Code* 1, 2, 25. Rätzinger 94.

[3] C. Ancyranum (314), can. 14, *Ss. Conc.* II, 526.

[4] C. Antiocheni (341), can. 24, *Ss. Conc.* II, 1327.

[5] C. Aurelianense III, (538) can. 12, *Ss. Conc.* IX, 15.

[6] C. Toletanum IV, (633) can. 33, *Ss. Conc.* X, 628.

[7] C. Aurelianense V (549), can. 13, *Ss. Conc.* IX, 131.

acquisitions;[1] while the Sixth Council of Paris was constrained to warn priests of the sacredness of property acquisitions and the care with which they were to be administered.[2]

As the property holdings of the Church increased in number and worth unconscionable laics frequently appropriated any portion they could conveniently purloin. Against these the Fathers and Councils inveighed with all the threats and punishments at their command. This was the Church's duty for it had acquired temporalities in a sort of trust to carry out the intentions of the donors and it could not allow such property to be diverted unjustly from its specified purpose. St. Augustine, seeing church goods appropriated by laics was constrained to warn his people that:—"He who thieves from the Church stands side by side with the castaway Judas."[3] The Councils were equally severe in their condemnation of this practice. Consequently laics were forbidden by the Fourth Synod of Rome to appropriate or alienate goods acquired by the Church.[4] The Council of Auvergne excommunicated those who usurped the property of the Church as this was considered as acquired for the support of the needy.[5] The Second Council of Toledo ruled that property stolen from the Church was to be restored.[6] Retainers of property belonging to the Church were declared excommunicated by the Third Council of Arles.[7] Violators of church goods were under excommunication until the stolen property was restored and complete satisfaction made according to the Fourth Council of Arles.[8] Unjust possessors of ecclesiastical goods were separated from communion with the Church by an enactment of the Third Council of Paris;[9] and those who after a warning persisted in defrauding the poor by retaining church goods were excommunicated and anathematized by the Second Council of Tours.[10]

During the Carlovingian period the Church continued to

---

[1] C. Nicaeni II, (787), can. 12, *Ss. Conc.* XIII, 432.

[2] C. Parisiense VI (829), can. 14, *Ss. Conc.* XIV, 549.

[3] St. Augustinus, *In Evang. Joann.*, Tract. L, c. 10, MPL, XXXIV, 1762. *Nicene and Post-Nicene Fathers* (First Series), VII, 281.

[4] Synodus Romanus IV (502), can. 4, *Ss. Conc.* VII,266.

[5] C. Arvernense (535), can. 5, *Ss. Conc.* VIII, 860.

[6] C. Toletanum II, (531), can. 4, *Ss. Conc.* VIII, 786.

[7] C. Aurelianense III (538), can. 22, *Ss. Conc.* IX, 18.

[8] C. Aurelianense IV (541), can. 25, *Ss. Conc.* IX, 117.

[9] C. Parisiense III (557), can. 1, *Ss. Conc.* IX, 744.

[10] C. Turonense II (567) can. 24, *Ss. Conc.* IX, 803.

acquire property by means of donations, taxes and testaments. Violations of such property became less frequent due to the efficient cooperation of Christian emperors with the Church and the fact that the temporal holdings of the Church were much reduced by the fall of Rome.[1]

With the return of more prosperous economic conditions in the twelfth and thirteenth centuries the Church again acquired considerable amounts of property from tributes and donations. It was at this time that vast incomes accrued to different ecclesiastical institutions from the tithe system. As the possessions of the Church increased avaricious laics began to appropriate ecclesiastical property. Perceiving the imminent danger that such flagrant violations of law would have upon the whole Church the Third Lateran Council (1179) forbade laics to acquire new tithes or to transfer to other laics tithes which they held.[2] In the Fourth Lateran Council (1215) many similar statutes—enunciating the Church's right to acquire tithes to the exclusion of all others—were sanctioned, but no formal decree was directed against the usurpers of ecclesiastical goods.[3] Similarly Boniface VIII in his noted Constitution "Clericis laicos"[4] threatened with excommunication those who violated property once acquired by the Church. Such timely enactments of Popes and Councils established the Church's right of acquisition and abated the evil of property usurpation. In certain quarters, however, abuses continued as is evident from similar legislation in succeeding councils.[5]

From the thirteenth to the sixteenth century the problem of property acquisition became difficult of settlement and was mooted among learned and unlearned alike. Temporal princes in addition to expropriating church goods and scheming to secure ecclesiastical emoluments sought to restrict the Church's right to acquire property; while on the other hand unscrupulous prelates sometimes levied all but insupportable burdens upon the faithful.[6]

It is indeed true that the Church acquired great amounts of

---

[1] *Benedicti Diaconi Capitulariorum Collectio*, MPL, XCVI, 725. *Francorum Regum Capitularia*, Can. III, Hludivici Regis, MPL, CXXXVIII, 582.

[2] C. 19, X, *de decimis, primitiis et oblationibus*, III, 30.

[3] C. 12, X, *de rebus ecclesiae alienandis vel non*, III, 13.

[4] C. 3, *de immunitate*, III, 23 in VI°.

[5] C. 13, *de electione electi potestate*, I, 6 in VI°. C. 2, *de rebus ecclesiae non alienandis* III, 9 in VI°.

[6] C. un., *de censibus, exactionibus et procurationibus*, III, 10 in VI°.

temporal goods during this period; but it must be borne in mind that vast property holdings were necessary for the Church. The Church's activities were greater than at any previous time. Bishops, for instance, often held the position of temporal rulers of high rank. They needed protection and assistance for the administration of justice and extensive properties for the continuance of their charitable enterprises. All this necessitated vast revenues.

Since the Church's property holdings became rather extensive at this time some radical thinkers formulated the opinion that the Church would be more effective in its work if it were shorn of all temporalities. This error later resolved itself into an unqualified denial by Marsilius of Padua, Jean de Jandun and Arnold of Brescia of even the Church's abstract right to acquire any property. They averred that absolute poverty without any right or claim to acquire temporalities was the original doctrine of Christ.[1] These teachings, as is patent to any student of history, were subtle and insidious ruses whereby unconscionable men sought to enrich themselves with Church property. Against them Pope John XXII directed two decrees in which the Church's right to acquire was clearly asserted by showing that the right of acquisition and ownership belonged to Christ and the Apostles. This right in turn was vested in their successors and could not therefore be violated or vilified by unscrupulous men.[2] A century later the Council of Constance condemned similar errors of the Hussites and Wycliffites. They advanced the doctrine that civil authorities could with impunity appropriate ecclesiastical property without any guilt of sacrilege, that ecclesiastical persons could not acquire temporal goods without incurring the guilt of sin and that the donors of ecclesiastical goods were seduced by Satan.[3]

3. After the Council of Trent.

The Council of Trent enacted stringent legislation relating to temporalities with the purpose of eradicating two abuses: the covetous tendencies of some members of the clergy and the refusal of laics to support the Church. Bishops were forbidden

[1] Wernz III, n. 146. Rivet, *Institutiones Iuris Eccles. Privati*, II, 13.

[2] Joannes XXII, const., *Cum inter nonnullos*, 13 Nov. 1323; Denz-Bann. n. 494–500. Joannes XXII, const., *Licet*, 23 Oct. 1327, *Fontes* n. 38.

[3] Martinus V, const., *Inter cunctas*, 22 Febr. 1418, *Fontes*, n. 43. Denz.-Bann. 598, 684–686.

to accept any fees for acts in any way associated with Ordination;[1] prelates were warned against imposing unnecessary or exorbitant exactions;[2] Regulars were restricted in soliciting alms;[3] priests were strictly forbidden to traffic in Mass stipends in any covetous manner.[4] The object of these and similar rulings was to check avaricious churchmen in their desire to acquire unnecessary temporalities for themselves or for the Church.

Laics, on the other hand, were reprehended by the Council for failure to support the Church. Some were tardy in giving tithes; others refused to give, while still others denied the Church's right to acquire tithes at all. Consequently severe reprimands and even ecclesiastical penalties were directed against them.[5]

In post-Tridentine times the exercise of the Church's right to acquire property was opposed by the Regalists, Gallicans, Josephists, French Revolutionists and others who sought to exalt the rights of civil rulers unreasonably by the sacrifice of the rights of individuals and the Church.[6] Likewise at various times and in different countries, as will be pointed out later, the Church was unable to acquire property rightfully belonging to it because of mortmain statutes or similar restrictions.

With the growth of states and the spirit of national consciousness in the eighteenth and nineteenth centuries the Church was frequently deprived of its rights to acquire property. Some states felt that as their power and control increased they acquired an indefeasible right to everything within grasp. The state was considered absolutely supreme with the right to make all other institutions servilely subservient to its own ends.[7] In such countries as France, Italy and Prussia the Church's rights to acquire property were flagrantly jeopardized and violated. Against such undue exaltation of State's rights the Church protested with uncompromising firmness. Thus Pius IX defended the Church's right to acquire and possess property in many authoritative pro-

---

[1] Conc. Trident., sess. XXI, *de ref.*, c. 1.

[2] Conc. Trident., sess. XXIV, *de ref.*, c. 3, 13.

[3] Conc. Trident., sess. XXI, *de ref.*, c. 9.

[4] Conc. Trident., sess. XXII, *Decretum de observandis et evitandis in celebratione Missae.*

[5] Conc. Trident. sess. XXII, *de ref.*, c. 11. Conc. Trident., sess. XXV, *de ref.*, c. 12.

[6] Pius V, const., *Admonet nos*, 29 Martii 1567, *Fontes*, n. 120. Urbanus VIII, const., *Sacrosancti*, 30 Sept. 1623, *Fontes* n. 203. Gregorius XVI, allocut., *Afflictas*, 1 Martii 1841, *Fontes* n. 496.

[7] Laski, *Grammar of Politics*, London, (1925), 44–50, 97–100.

nouncements.[1] Protestations were likewise made by Pius X and Pius XI when the Church's rights to acquire and possess property were violated in France, Mexico, and other countries.[2]

The principal modes of acquiring ecclesiastical property at the present day are:—tithes, first-fruits, alms, the cathedraticum, charitable subsidy, special fees, prescription, grants, bequests and last wills. The Church has not only the right but even the duty to protect its right to acquire property by all just means of the natural and positive law allowed to others. Moreover, it has the concomitant right and duty to protect property once acquired from all unjust encroachments of the state. Should the state interfere unjustly it would violate a sacred right of the Church as clearly enunciated in the Constitution of Clement XIII.[3]

[1] Pius IX, allocut. *Quibus luctuosissimis*, 5 Sept. 1851, *Fontes*, n. 512. Pius IX, allocut, *Numquam fore*, 15 Dec. 1856, *Fontes*, n. 522. Pius IX, ep. encycl., *Quanta cura*, 8 Dec. 1864, *Fontes* n. 542. Pius IX, Syllabus errorum, prop. 26, 27. *Fontes* n. 543.

[2] Pius X, ep. *Acre nefariumque*, 14 Maii 1905, *Fontes* n. 668. Pius X, allocut, *Gravissimum*, 21 Febr. 1906, *Fontes* n. 672. Pius X, litt. encycl. *Iamdudum*, 24 Maii 1911, *Fontes* n. 692. Pius XI, litt. encycl. *Iniquis afflictisque*, 18 Nov. 1926, AAS, XVIII, 465.

[3] Clemens XIII, const., *Alias ad Apostolatus*, 30 Jan. 1768, *Fontes*, n. 464.

CHAPTER II.

Historico-Juridical Development.

The Church's right to acquire temporal goods freely and independently of any civil power is generally recognized today. It is true that this right has been impugned at times in theory and practice, especially during periods of national excitement and delusion; but wherever the sane principles of equity and justice are recognized there also the Church's rights are safeguarded. Christ and His Apostles acquired temporal goods. This right has passed down to their lawfully constituted successors not from any generous grant of a civil ruler but from the inherent nature of the Church as an organized, perfect, visible and necessary society as enunciated by Boniface VIII in his celebrated constitution "Unam sanctam."[1]

No one questions the natural right of individuals to acquire and hold property. Similarly the individual has a right to group with other individuals in the formation of a society or corporation, provided this be not subversive to the common good.[2] As the individual, so also groups of individuals lawfully organized, have the right to acquire property.[3] Likewise the societies thus formed have the obligation and necessity of supporting themselves, and doing this honestly and justly by paying the expenses they incur, by furthering their works and aims and finally by supporting any members who are in need of assistance. Now, if other corporations and societies enjoy rights to acquire property for a far greater reason should the Church's rights be recognized and protected by all nations that have a regard for

---

[1] C. 1, *de maioritate et obedientia*, I, 8, in Extravag. com. Wernz III n. 135. Sanguineti 329. LeCroix II, 3, 2, nota 1. Solmi, *Storia del Diritto Italiano*, 506. For fuller treatment of this particular subject consult the scholarly dissertation of Rev. Dr. C. J. Bartlett, *The Tenure of Parochial Property in the United States*.

[2] Cavagnis III, n. 377. Maroto I, 458–464. Savigny-Scialoja II, 279.

[3] Leo XIII, ep. encycl. *Immortale Dei*, 1 Nov. 1885, *Fontes* n. 492. Leo XIII, litt. encycl. *Rerum novarum*, 15 maii, 1891, *Fontes* n. 611.

justice. The Church has higher motives and worthier ideals than the ordinary corporation; its history proves that it is beneficial to mankind; its work is necessary for the guidance and uplift of human society; it accomplishes more for the individual and society in general than the ordinary corporation. In return it in truth merits the world's gratitude. If it does not receive this; it at least insists on justice.[1]

It is an established fact that the Church acquired temporal goods from the first centuries. History and Scripture attest that from Apostolic times collections were taken up among the faithful, that landed property was donated to the Church, all of which was carefully administered for the clergy and the poor.[2] Under some title or other the Christians acquired such property as churches and cemeteries.[3] The cemetery entrusted to the care of Callistus by Pope Zephyrinus (198) must have belonged to the Catholic community as cemeteries were usually considered to be the joint possession of the faithful.[4] In 222 Alexander Severus decided in favor of the Christians when a lawsuit for property arose between them and certain shop-keepers. In 253 the Emperor Valerian published a decree whereby he sought to close the subterranean retreats of the Christians by forbidding them either to hold assemblies or to enter those places which they called their cemeteries. In 272 the Emperor Aurelian settled a dispute between the Catholic community at Antioch and Paul of Samosata, the latter being evicted from the Bishop's house.[5] During the persecution of Diocletian the cemeteries of the Christians were confiscated.[6] All these facts establish proofs that the Church acquired temporalities from the time of its inception.

This much is clear and unchallenged. It is difficult, however, to ascertain in what precise person the proprietary rights of the

---

[1] C. 3, *de immunitate ecclesiarum*, III, 23 in VI°. C. 1, *de maioritate et obedientia*, I, 8 in Extravag. com.

[2] Acts IV:32. Eusebius, *Historia Ecclesiae*, VIII, 2; MPG, XX, 743; X, 2, MPG, XX, 846. St. Cyprianus, *De opere et eleemosynis*, c. 25, MPL, IV, 643. *Code*, 1, 3. Uhlhorn 309.

[3] DeRossi, *Bulletino di archeologia cristiana*, (1867) 46. Leclercq, *Manual d'Archeologie Chretienne*, I, 323. Lanciani, *Pagan and Christian Rome*, 111.

[4] Tertullianus, *Liber ad Scapulam*, 3, MPL, I, 782. Tertullianus, *De anima*, c. 50, MPL, I, 779.

[5] Eusebius, *Historia Ecclesiae*, VII, 30, MPG, XX, 710. Lactantius, *De mortibus persecutorum*, c. XII, MPL, VII, 214.

[6] Eusebius, *Historia Ecclesiae*, VII, 13, MPG, XX, 674; VIII, 2, MPG, XX, 743.

Church were vested and by what protection or legal recognition the Church held temporalities once they were acquired. This is important and relevant here because the corporation enjoying proprietary rights was vested with the right to acquire. During the periods of the persecutions the Church was proscribed by law as an organization inimical to the Roman Empire;[1] to hold property at all the Christians may have formed themselves into corporations similar to the burial or mutual-aid associations so common among the Romans;[2] or they may have been recognized under the title of a religious corporation which, though illicit, could have been tolerated except during the times of persecution.[3] Either system would have sufficiently protected the interests of the Church during times of peace; while neither would have safeguarded its property during the persecutions with law and public opinion decidedly adverse to all things Christian.[4]

From the earliest times of Roman Law there existed clubs and trade-guilds of some sort.[5] In the first period of law these did not possess complete corporate capacity for the property belonged to the individual members and not to the association as such. Ancient Roman law had no definite concepts of the existence of an artificial person enjoying proprietary rights.[6] Gradually the conception of an artificial or juridical person with rights and obligations was evolved. At the time of the Empire public corporations with full proprietary rights came into being; and at a somewhat later date private corporations, fashioned after public corporations, were recognized by law.[7] The property of such corporations was the property not of the several persons, but of a single person: the corporation as such. In other words the corporation, the collective whole, was regarded as a new and different person, as an individual unit distinct from the individuals

---

[1] Duchesne 280.

[2] *Digest* 47, 22, 1. Tertullianus, *Apologia* 39, MPL, I, 470. Tertullianus, *De anima*, c. 50, MPL, I, 782. DeRossi, *Roma sotterranea cristiana*, I, 100. DeRossi, *Bullettino di archeologia cristiana*, (1864), 28, 57; (1865), 90. Marucchi, I, 119. Sagmueller, *Kirchenrecht*, 764. Mommsen, *History of Rome*, V, 11. Uhlhorn, 141. Ferrini, n. 72–78. Fac-similes of charters and by-laws of such *collegia* are reproduced in Bruns, *Fontes Iuris Romani Antiqui*, 345–356.

[3] Duchesne 278–280. Marucchi I, 123–125.

[4] *Digest* 47, 2, 2; Sherman II, §547.

[5] *Digest* 3, 4, 1 pr.; 49, 14; Code 10, 1. Mommsen, *History of Rome*, II, 8. Savigny-Scialoja, *Sistema del diritto romano attuale*, II, 257.

[6] Sohm-Ledlie 187.

[7] *Digest*, 3, 4, 1, 1. Baldwin, *Modern Political Instituions*, 142. Savigny-Scialoja,·II, 258. Pacchioni, II, 258.

that made up the corporation. This collective whole, this organized and unified body of members living and acting by means of a corporate personality and constitution became a new subject of rights and duties distinct from the individuals.[1] Hence the chief characteristics of such corporations were twofold: they possessed a personality entirely distinct from the natural persons who comprised them; and enjoyed existence beyond the natural period of human life. These elements of corporate life fitted in eminently well with the Church's exigencies for its dioceses and parishes needed a legal life that would survive bishops and priests and at the same time safeguard property rights against individual dissenters and schismatics.

The Roman law on corporations and the proprietary rights of such corporations is generally clear. There are two obscure points, however, that render difficult the application and adjustment of Roman law to the organization of the Church in the first centuries. It is not clear from the extant sources whether the approbation of the state was necessary for every corporation. Some writers maintain that the state alone could endow a group with juristic and corporate life; while others hold that the right of individuals to group themselves into corporations is innate and natural and hence is not dependant upon the state for juridical personality. According to this opinion recognition might have been necessary for the licit organization of a society, but it was not an essential condition for validity.[2] If corporate life, in accordance with the first view, really depended upon state recognition then it can be safely surmised that Church corporations could hardly have existed as such for any protracted period of time during the first centuries because of the frequency of persecutions. If legal recognition were not necessary for corporate life, Church organizations could have flourished and enjoyed proprietary rights during times of peace. During the persecutions they would have been considered illegal because of an illicit existence or purpose.

A second difficulty that tended to obscure the precise determination of the juristic personality acquiring property in the Church arose from the peculiar provisions of Roman law govern-

---

[1] *Digest,* 1, 8, 6, 1; 3, 4, 7, 1; 36, 1, 1, 15.

[2] *Digest,* 47, 22, 1-3. Ferrini, n. 73. Savigny-Scialoja III, 169. Bonfante, *Istituzione,* §19.

ing "res iuris divini."[1] The objects considered of divine law and consequently not subject to human ownership were temples, burial places and holy things.[2] They constituted a class apart, reserved from the exercise of ownership, and were very often thought to be the possession of the gods although strictly speaking the property was considered as excluded from private ownership rather than belonging to any juristic person or deity.[3] Perhaps it was in imitation of this unique juridical constitution that Jesus Christ, the martyrs and saints were oftentimes considered as legal property-holders of goods acquired by the Church.[4] No doubt it was this that lead Navarrus (Martin de Azpilcueta)[5] and Donatus[6] to formulate the opinion that God, Christ or a saint was the subject in whom ecclesiastical ownership was vested. At present this theory is rightly rejected in Canon 1499 § 2, for if Christ and the saints were the true proprietors of Church goods they would in like manner be held to obligations and debts; and this would be preposterous. God, it is true, is the supreme lord of all temporalities but He has beneficently bestowed the secondary dominion of these upon men.

Until the Church was recognized by Roman law in the fourth century the property acquired by it was in a precarious state. It was preyed upon by individuals and municipalities with little or no hope of redress or restitution. There are, it is true, records of a few instances when property of the Christians was protected but these were among the isolated cases where justice was meted out regardless of the prejudices against the Church.[7]

In 311 A.D. Galerius reluctantly permitted the Christians to practice their religion in virtue of his Edict of Toleration. This did not, however, restore confiscated property nor did it assure to the Christians all rights of citizenship. The clause "provided they do nothing contrary to good order" was capable of interpretations extremely adverse to Christians. This vague uncertainty was banished and the jeopardy to which the faithful had been exposed was abolished by the Decree of Milan in 313.[8] This Decree

[1] Gaius, 2, 4. Sohm-Ledlie, 302. Moyle 195.

[2] Sherman II, §560.

[3] Sohm-Ledlie, 189. Colquhoun §926. Savigny-Scialoja II, 269.

[4] Rivet II, 21. Wernz III, 138.

[5] *De reditibus ecclesiasticis*, q. 1, monit, 40, opp. 1.

[6] *Rerum regularium praxis resolutoria*, I, 2, 14, q. 27.

[7] Lactantius, *De mortibus persecutorum*, c. 12, MPL, VII, 214.

[8] Eusebius, *Historia ecclesiae*, X, 5, MPG, XX, 883. Kirch, *Enchiridion Fontium Historiae Eccleiasticae* n. 352–353.

clearly enunciated the Church's rights and guaranteed their future recognition in Roman law: "Listening to the demands of both public welfare and sound reason, we have thought it our duty to enact that leave shall be refused to no one whatever who has given his heart either to the teachings of the Christians or to that kind of religion which he himself feels to be the most suitable to him; so that the Supreme Divinity, worshipped by us with full freedom, may be able to show to us in all things its wonted favor and benevolence. . . .[1] All restrictions which are contained in former instructions concerning the Christians . . . are all and entirely cancelled; and that each and everyone desirous to observe the religion of the Christians may do so without any fear, and without any disadvantage to himself. . . . As to the Christians we deem it our duty to issue still another enactment, concerning the places in which they formerly were accustomed to assemble, and about which a well-known rule was laid down in the communications sent heretofore to thy Fidelity. Those persons who appear to have bought these identical places either from our treasury or from anybody else shall restore the same to the Christians without money and without charging any price, setting aside all deception and delay. Likewise those who have received them as presents shall immediately surrender them to the same Christians. . . . And since the Christians, as is well known, possessed not only those places where they used to meet, but also others which belonged not to individuals but to them as corporations, that is to the churches, we comprise all these in the aforesaid ordinance (of restitution)." This decree indubitably shows that the property acquired by the Church before the time of Constantine was considerable. It is to be further noted that only Church property was to be restored; the private property of Christians was not included.

In 321 A. D. another right of the Church was recognized and safeguarded, namely that of acquiring property by testament.[2] This right was later amplified and interpreted by Justinian who decided that the institution of Jesus Christ as heir is to be under-

[1] For a discussion of the problem of the actual existence and promulgation of the Edict of Milan, confer Knipfing, J. R., *Catholic Historical Review*, (1925) IV, 483–503; Knipfing, J. R. *Revue Belge de Philogie etd' Historia*, (1922) I, 693–705; Knipfing, J. R., *Das angelbliche Mailander Edict v. J. 313 im Lichte der neueren Forschung*, Zeitschrift für Kirchengeschichte, 1922, 206–218.

[2] *Theod. Code* 16, 2, 4.

stood to indicate the church of the testator's residence; an archangel or martyr, the church of his place of residence so dedicated; failing which, that so dedicated in the metropolis of the province; and should there be many so dedicated, that to which the testator showed a preference in his lifetime; and in default of such, the poorer.[1]

In Justinianean law the legal constitution of the Church became clear and determined. It was recognized as a corporation and hence could acquire property as other corporate bodies.[2] It was distinct in many respects from the ordinary corporations of Roman law, principally in virtue of the foundations or institutions that partook in a certain measure of its legal life. It also enjoyed more privileges than the ordinary corporation.[3] The property and affairs of the corporations were controlled and administered principally by bishops in union with the Church assisted by economes of their choice.[4] The importance of the bishop in property matters is easily inferred from an epistle ascribed to Pope Urban:—"They began to consign to the mother churches the property and lands which they were wont to sell. The property moreover in the possession of the several parishes was left in the hands of the bishops, who hold the place of the Apostles; and it is to this day and ought to be so in the future."[5] The legislation of the councils insisted that property acquired by the Church had to be retained in sacred trust under the direction of the bishop.[6]

The bishop's powers over property acquired by and for the Church were very extensive during the early centuries.[7] Freewill offerings were made to him, through him the Church accepted donations, grants and legacies; and in law he was constituted executor of wills.[8] The bulk of all such church goods was divided into four portions according to a custom which Pope Simplicius

---

[1] *Code* 1, 2, 25; 1, 3, 46. Savigny-Scialoja, II, 269–273.

[2] *Code*, 1, 2, 1; 1, 2, 22; 1, 2, 14, 2; 6, 48, 10.

[3] *Code* 1, 2.

[4] C. Chalcedonensis (451), actionis XV, can. 26, *Ss. Conc.* VII, 367.

[5] *Ante-Nicene Fathers*, VIII, 619.

[6] C. Ancyranum (314), can. 14, *Ss. Conc.* II, 526. C. Chalcedonensis (451), actionis XV, can. 26, *Ss. Conc.* VII, 367.C. Nicaeni II (787), can. 12, *Ss. Conc.* XIII, 432. C. Parisiense VI, (829), can. 14, *Ss. Conc.* XIV, 549.

[7] C. Antiochenum (341), can. 25, *Ss. Conc.* II, 1328. C. Chalcedonensis (451), actionis VI, can. 2, *Ss. Conc.* VII, 175. C. Cabilonense (649), can. 14, *Ss. Conc.* X, 1192. C. Toletanum (633), can. 33, *Ss. Conc.* X, 628.

[8] *Code*, 1, 3, 45.

(468–483) called ancient: one portion for the bishop and his household; another for the clergy; another for the poor and the fourth for the repairs of the churches.[1]

As the Church spread into sparsely settled countries the lineaments of its former system of property acquisition gradually changed. Churches in villages and outlying districts could not acquire revenues and donations sufficient to support a bishop, his clergy and household. Still the people in these localities needed someone to minister to their spiritual wants. Hence parish priests were appointed to take care of souls under the jurisdiction of the bishops and to secure the temporal goods necessary for religious purposes.[2] The bishops, in virtue of their office, retained the right and duty of supervising the means by which ecclesiastical goods were acquired even though the newly formed parish churches were considered separate entities in law.[3]

At times the poverty of the faithful was such that they could not afford donations for building and keeping in repair churches necessary for divine worship. In cases like this lords and wealthy land-owners often donated the ground, built the churches, kept them in repair and even paid the salary of the attending clergymen.[4] Thus began the system of benefices and ecclesiastical patronage with the patron's right of advowson. During the Middle Ages most of the churches were endowed by such patrons. The system of patronage, though in many respects a blessing for the spreading of the faith throughout Europe, became the cause of many abuses, such as the expropriation of tithes by laymen and the simoniacal appointment to benefices.[5] The stricter legislation of the last centuries and especially that of the Code has done much to obviate the dangers of this system.

In the United States the acquisition and tenure of Church

---

[1] C. Bracarense II, (563), cap. VII, *Ss. Conc.* IX, 778. C. Triburiense, (891), can. 13, *Ss. Conc.* XVIII[a], 140. Can. III, *Hludowici Regis*, MPL CXXXVIII, 582. Ven. Beda, *Ecclesiae Historia*, I, 27, MPL, XCV, 58. Thomassinus, III, 2, 12. Oftentimes church goods are referred to as divided into three portions. In both cases the actual apportionment remains practically the same, only the terminology being different.

[2] S. Zorell, *De origine paroeciarum*, Archiv. für K. K. R., LXXXII, (1902), 75.

[3] C. 16, 19, C. XII, q. 1. C. 68, C. XVI, q. 1.

[4] *Novellae*, 57, 2. C. Bracarense II, (563), can. 6, *Ss. Conc.* IX, 778. C. 1, 2, 4, 6, C.X, q.1. C. 1, C. XVI, q. 5; c. 31, 32, 37, C. XVI, q. 7. C. 5, 16, X, *de jure patronatus*, III, 38.

[5] A. MacDonald, *Decadence of Faith and the Ecclesiastical Benefice*, *Ecclesiastical Review*, LXXII, (1925), 254.

property have varied according to the laws of the different states. The Thirteen Colonies, with the exception of Maryland, enacted penal statutes against Catholics. Consequently Church property was legally and publicly acquired and held as such in only two colonies: in Maryland during the first period of its history because of Lord Baltimore's influence, and in Pennsylvania because of the non-enforcement of an act of 1730 against Catholics. In the Colonies the property acquired by the Church was held in fee simple. The titles to the property were held by the individual priest and transferred from one missionary to another by will or deed.

In virtue of the first amendment to our Constitution religious freedom is guaranteed to all denominations, although no religion is recognized as the state religion.[1] Hence some form of incorporation was necessary for the Church in order to hold the property it acquired. The right of determining the regulations for the tenure of property was left to the individual States. In some States there were no explicit laws; in others doubtful statutes confused lawyers and churchmen. Generally each congregation with the knowledge and sanction of the bishop petitioned the state legislature for recognition as a body corporate. Lay trustees were generally chosen as members of the body corporate. In the beginning this system appeared to solve the Church's problem of holding property safely and at the same time of allowing lay members privileges consonant with the democratic principles upon which our government was founded. Despite auspicious beginnings the trustee system resulted disastrously and had to be opposed by the hierarchy, especially Bishop England and Archbishop Hughes.[2] The evils of the system became so widespread that Pope Pius VII was constrained to issue a brief, *Non sine magno*,[3] reprobating the immoderate claims of the trustees in the temporal affairs that pertained by right and law to the bishops.[4] In brief the principle involved was that property acquired by the Church belongs to the Church and is not to be interfered with in any way. The modes of acquisition and the means of holding property once acquired are determined by the authorized prelates of the Church and not by a group of laics.

[1] Norton, *Constitution of the United States*, 197.

[2] *Bishop England's Works*, (Baltimore, 1849), V. 109–213. Hughes, *Works*, (New York, 1864), I, 548–632.

[3] 24 Aug. 1822, *Fontes*, n. 480.

[4] Pius VII, *litt. ad Episcopos Americ. Sept.*, 24 Aug. 1822, *Coll.* 773.

Alarmed by the abuses that followed in the wake of the trustee system the hierarchy of the country adopted a method of holding Church property that went to the other extreme. This was called fee simple, in virtue of which the bishop was considered in the eyes of the civil law as the sole owner of the property vested in his name. This was a precarious and exceptional method adopted with the avowed purpose of protecting church property in the critical struggle with the trustee system.[1] With the return of peaceful times in the Church most of the property was incorporated as corporation sole or corporation aggregate as suggested by the Third Plenary of Baltimore,[2] and the S. Congregation of the Council in an Instruction to the American Bishops in 1911.[3] The modes of acquisition of Church property were not affected by the different systems of tenure. The faithful contributed with commendable generosity at all times. They knew that their donations and tributes would be conscientiously employed in the furthering of Christ's mission on earth.

---

[1] I. Prov. Conc. Baltimorensis, (1829).
[2] n. 267–269.
[3] *Ecclesiastical Review*, XLV, (1911), 585.

CHAPTER III.

Church's Rights of Property Acquisition.

1. Vindication of Church's Right to Acquire Property.

Canon 1495.

§ 1. Ecclesia catholica et Apostolica Sedes nativum ius habent libere et independenter a civili potestate acquirendi, retinendi et administrandi bona temporalia ad fines sibi proprios prosequendos.

Canon 1495, § 1, enunciates the Church's right to acquire property in language that has been used in decrees and condemnations in the Church's century-long conflict with heretics and usurpers of ecclesiastical goods. Similar declarations of the Church's rights have been made at different times against the errors of Arnold of Brescia, the Waldenses, Marsilius of Padua, Jean de Jandun[1] and Wycliffe who taught that the Church's acquisition of temporal goods was forbidden by Christ;[2] as well as against the Gallicans and regalists who held that the Church had not an inherent right to temporalities, but acquired it by the arbitrary concession of civil authorities.[3] The Council of Constance and Pope Martin V condemned several Wycliffean propositions which impugned the Church's right to temporal goods;[4] while Pius IX in his Syllabus of condemned propositions[5] and his Consistorial Allocution, *Quibus luctuosissimis*, virtually formulated the language employed by the Code.[6]

---

[1] Marsilius of Padua and Jean de Jandun, who were professors of the University of Paris and the most important literary antagonists of the Popes in their day, published the celebrated *Defensor Pacis* in 1326. Pastor, I, 76.

[2] Wernz III, 135. Solmi 723.

[3] Rivet, II, 14. P. Fourneret, *Biens Ecclesistique, Dict. de Theol. Cath.* II, p. 1, col. 865.

[4] Prop. 10, 32, 36. *Fontes*, n. 43.

[5] Prop. 26, 27, *Fontes* n. 543.

[6] 5 Sept. 1851, *Fontes*, n. 512. Vide etiam: Pius IX, allocut. *Nunquam fore*, 15 Dec. 1856, *Fontes* n. 522. Pius IX, ep. encycl. *Incredibili*, 17 Sept. 1863, *Fontes* n. 537. Pius X, ep. *Acre nefariumque*, 14 Maii 1905, *Fontes* n. 668.Pius X, ep. encycl. *Vehementer Nos*, 11, Feb. 1906, *Fontes* n. 671. Pius X, allocut. *Gravissimum*, 21 Feb. 1906, *Fontes* n. 672. Pius X, litt. encycl. *Une fois encore*, 6 Jan. 1907, *Fontes* n. 677. Pius X, litt. encycl. *Iamdudum*, 24 Maii 1911, *Fontes* n. 692.

In Canon 1495 the term "Catholic Church" is understood to mean the visible and perfect society founded by Christ and instituted as a juridical person.[1] The "Apostolic See" according to Canon 7 includes not only the Roman Pontiff but the Roman Curia as well, consisting of the congregations, tribunals and offices.[2] The Church has an "innate right," that is a right proceeding from its very nature as founded by Christ. It has received this right of acquiring goods from Him whose authority gave it existence; and Christ alone established it in such a manner that the possession and use of temporal goods are necessary.[3] The Church enjoys the "free and independent" right of exercising its legitimate prerogatives so long as these are just and equitable. Hence its rights are not to be infringed upon by the state, which has neither an absolute nor unlimited right to temporal goods.[4] The right of the state cannot be absolute for God alone is the Supreme Lord of the universe; nor can it be unlimited for the state has a right to temporal goods only in so far as they are necessary for the pursuit of its own ends without losing sight of or disregarding the rights of others.[5] The ends of the Church and State being different, there can be no conflict so long as neither transgresses the limits of its proper sphere.[6] Within the last centuries the transgressions on the part of civil powers have been frequent. Even in our own country restraining measures have been passed against the Church's right of property acquisition, which were ill in accord with the full measure of religious liberty usually granted.[7] This discrimination against the Church was protested against by the Fathers of the Second Plenary Council of Baltimore.[8]

Other nations have at times exceeded the limits of their powers by violating the Church's rights of acquisition by enact-

---

[1] Canon 100 §1.

[2] Vermeersch-Creusen, II, n. 817. Cocchi VI, 332.

[3] Cocchi VI, 331.

[4] Clemens XIII, const. *Alias ad Apostolaius*, 30 Jan. 1768, *Fontes* n. 464. Leo XIII, litt. encycl. *Immortale Dei*, 1 Nov. 1885, *Fontes* n. 592. *Acta et decreta Conc. Plen. Latinae Americae*, n. 825. Laski, *Grammar of Politics*, 97.

[5] Palmieri, *Tractatus de Romano Pontifice*, 121. Mazzella, *De Religione et Ecclesia* 440.

[6] Laski, *Grammar of Politics*, 134.

[7] L. Johnston, *Religious Liberty in the United States*, *Catholic University Bulletin*, IX, (1903), 61.

[8] II Plen. Council of Baltimore, *Pastoral Letters*, p. cix.

ing iniquitous statutes of mortmain.[1] These restraining measures originated during the feudal period primarily because the kings and feudal lords wished to limit the Church in its property holdings which were considered a menace to their power, and partly because the extensive ownership of land by ecclesiastical corporations was interpreted as inconsistent with feudal tenure. The earliest measure relating to mortmain was an edict of the Emperor Frederick Barbarossa in 1158 prohibiting certain conveyances to Church corporations.[2] In 1279 and 1285 drastic legislation was enacted in England to deprive the Church of its capacity to inherit and alienate property.[3] Similar legislation[4] remained in force in England to the end of the last century. Laws fashioned after the English statutes were enacted in other European countries during the reigns of Maximilian I, Ferdinand II, Leopold I, Maria Theresa and Joseph II.[5]

Owing to the absence of great religious corporations in this country and to the fact that the feudal system antedated this Republic the mortmain statutes were not re-enacted in the United States, with the possible exception of Pennsylvania. In 1832 the supreme court of that State declared that the mortmain statutes had been extended to the State "only in so far as they prohibit dedications of property to superstitious uses and grants to corporations without a statutory license." Just what effect this had in actual practice is not agreed upon by lawyers.[6] Although the mortmain statutes have been held generally not to be in force in the United States as a part of the common law still their influence is felt in a vague way and is responsible to some extent for laws restricting the amount of property which a religious corporation may take and hold,[7] or prohibiting all devises for religious purposes unless made at a time prior to a designated time before the death of the testator.[8]

---

[1] C. 1, *de maioritate et obedientia*, I, 8 in Extravag. com. Cavagnis III, 221. Schupfer 321.

[2] Solmi, 570, 724.

[3] 7 Edward I, 13, *De viris religiosis*. 13 Edward I, 32. 18 Edward I, 1. Pollock-Maitland, *History of English Law*, I, 315.

[4] 9 George II, 35. 51, 52 Victoria 42.

[5] Aichner 109.

[6] 1 Watts Reports 224. Holland v. Alcock, 108 N. Y. Court of Appeals Reports, 329.

[7] Bird v. Merklee, 144 N. Y. 544, 39 N. E. 645, 27 L. R. A. 423.

[8] Speer v. Colbert, 200 U. S. 130, 26 S. Ct. 201, 50 U. S. (L ed) 403. Davis v. Davis, 62 Ohio St. 411, 57 N. E. 317, 78 A. S. R. 725.

Mortmain statutes militated against the liberty and independence of the Church. They were a breach of commutative justice since the same rights or property acquisition and control ought to be accorded the Church as any private individual.[1] Some authors hold that a moderate application of the mortmain statutes is permissible wherever the Church's needs are well provided for.[2] This, however, cannot be considered as a valid reason; for following this line of argumentation a rich man could be despoiled of his goods simply and solely because he was blessed with an abundance of material resources.

2. Rights of Individual Churches to Acquire Property.

Canon 1495.

§ 2. Etiam ecclesiis singularibus aliisque personis moralibus quae ab ecclesiastica auctoritate in iuridicam personam erectae sint, ius est, ad normam sacrorum canonum, bona temporalia acquirendi, retinendi et administrandi.

Some such rule as is formulated in Canon 1495, § 2, was observed in practice from the earliest days of the Church. Individual parishes and other ecclesiastical corporations were cognizant of their capacity and right to acquire property.[3] Nevertheless they acknowledged an ecclesiastical superior to whom they were answerable for their acts of acquisition.[4] They likewise realized that their right to acquire rested on the grounds of their union in faith and discipline with the universal Church. Thus, for instance, Paul of Samosota, Bishop of Antioch, was deprived of this right because of his separation from the Church of Rome.[5]

Individual organizations or subordinate corporations in the Church derive their juristic personality in virtue of a prescript of law or a grant from a competent ecclesiastical superior, provided this be given by a formal decree and that the purpose of

---

[1] Clemens XIII, const. *Alias ad Apostolatus*, 30 Jan. 1768, *Fontes* n. 464 Cavagnis III, 221.

[2] Phillips, *Compendium Iuris Eccesiastici*, 408. Aichner 109.

[3] Eusebius, *Historia Ecclesiae*, X, 5. MPG, XX, 883. *Code*, 1, 2, 26,

[4] C. Ancyranum (314), can. 14, *Ss. Conc.* II, 526. C. Chalcedonensis (451), actionis XV, can. 26, *Ss. Conc.* VII, 367. C. Cabilonense (649), can. 14, *Ss. Conc.* X, 1192. C. Parisiense VI (829), can. 14, *Ss. Conc.* XIV, 549. C. 16, 19, C. XII, q. 1.

[5] Eusebius, *Historia Ecclesiae*, VII, 30, MPG. XX, 710.

the establishment be religious or charitable.[1] As is clear from the present law of the Church the granting of juristic personality to any ecclesiastical corporation is an act of jurisdiction in the external forum. Since priests cannot exercise this power parishes are not, strictly speaking, constituted with legal and ecclesiastical autonomy at the present time. They may, however, be sometimes considered as such for convenience.[2] In the first centuries nearly every parish had a bishop at its head. Hence individual and legally autonomous churches could have been more numerous than now.

Since union with the Apostolic See and the universal Church is a requisite for every subordinate religious corporation it follows that dissident parishes and schismatic corporations forfeit their right to acquire church property or to retain the property acquired while a corporate member of the Church. By schism they cease to be organic members of the fold; they lose their juridical entity according to Canon Law and their property reverts to the Church.[3] This same principle is enunciated by the Third Plenary Council of Baltimore: "Quaecumque sint in Ecclesia societates, vel congregationes, collegia vel ordines, sive laicorum sive religiosorum, bona temporalia, quae Ecclesiae nomine cohonestentur, acquirendi vel possidendi nec potestatem nec ius habent, nisi quia et quatenus sunt membra in uno Ecclesiae corpore. Quod tam verum est ut, si quae societas ecclesiastica ab obedientia Ecclesiae debita recesserit vel a fide Catholica apostataverit, nullo unquam titulo bona ecclesiastica quorum prius dominium habuit, sibi reclamare legitime possit. Scisso etenim unitatis ecclesiasticae vinculo, scinditur et titulus possessionis bonorum Ecclesiae, quae essentialiter una est."[4] The same principle is upheld in the courts of the United States where it is recognized that those who fall away from the faith can have no right to take away with them any of the property of the Church.[5] Property is donated to the Church or acquired by it in order to help the spread of the true faith of Christ. Hence, if

---

[1] Canon 100 §1. It must be noted that the aim be religious or charitable and not merely a humanly philanthropic one. Vermeersch-Creusen, *Summa Novi Iuris Canonici*, p. 172. Wernz III, n. 195. Cavagnis III, 365.

[2] Wernz III, 139. Vermeersch-Creusen II, 818. Augustine VI, 553.

[3] Bachhofen, *Summa Iuris Ecclesiastici Publici*, (Neo Eboraci), (1910), 43.

[4] *Conc. Plen. Baltimor. III Acta et Decreia*, n. 264.

[5] Dockhus v. Lithuanian Benefit Society of St. Anthony, Pa. 25, 29. Smith v. Pedigo, 145 Ind. 361, 424.

dissenters or schismatics undertake to disseminate different teachings and erroneous doctrines it would be preposterous and inequitable to allow them to share in the property manifestly intended for other purposes.[1]

3. Right of Church to Exact Means of Support.

Canon 1496.

Ecclesiae ius quoque est, independens a civili potestate, exigendi a fidelibus quae ad cultum divinum, ad honestam clericorum aliorumque ministrorum sustentationem et ad reliquos fines sibi proprios sint necessaria.

Since the Church as a perfect society has the inherent, free and independent right to acquire the temporal goods requisite for its work it must follow that the necessary means be possible of attainment.[2] All legitimately established societies may depend on their members for support and exact it from them. In like manner the Church claims the right of demanding contributions which will enable it to carry on religious worship, provide for its ministers and attain its own end. These the Church demands from the faithful who become its subjects by Baptism and determines what form the assistance will take and how to obtain it in complete independence from any civil power or other interference. That this is a right of the Church and in strict accord with its ancient teaching is evidenced by the proposition of the Synod of Pistoia which Pius VI condemned as false and rash: "Quasi turpis abusus crimine notandi essent ministri Ecclesiae, cum secundum receptum et probatum Ecclesiae morem et institutum utuntur iure promulgato ab apostolico accipiendi temporalia ab his, quibus spiritualia ministrantur."[3]

In proportion as the generosity of the faithful extends or restricts itself the Church must emphasize its right to exact taxes and tributes with greater or less insistence. Happily at the present time the faithful are very generous as a rule. Hence the Church's means of support are secured more by appeal and counsel than by command.[4]

---

[1] Page v. Corby, 41 Mass. 211. Harper v. Straw 52 Ky. 48. Hale v. Everett, 53 N. H. 9.

[2] Canon 1496.

[3] Const. *Auctorem fidei*, 28 Aug. 1794, Prop. 54, *Fontes* n. 475.

[4] Concilium Plenarium Americae Latinae, n. 829. Vermeersch-Creusen II, n. 817.

CHAPTER IV.

CLASSIFICATION OF ECCLESIASTICAL TEMPORALITIES

Canon 1497.

§ 1. Bona temporalia, sive corporalia, tum immobilia, tum mobilia, sive incorporalia, quae vel ad Ecclesiam universam et ad Apostolicam Sedem vel ad aliam in Ecclesia personam moralem pertineant, sunt *bona ecclesiastica.*

§ 2. Dicuntur *sacra,* quae consecratione vel benedictione ad divinum cultum destinata sunt; *pretiosa,* quibus notabilis valor sit, artis vel historiae vel materiae causa.

Following the distinctions of Roman law the property of the Church is considered as divided into corporeal, both movable and immovable, and incorporeal. Things were classified by the Romans as corporeal or incorporeal accordingly as they fell under or escaped the observation of the senses.[1] Movable goods comprise all those objects that can move or be moved from place to place without impairing their integrity; while immovable goods cannot be transferred from place to place without jeopardizing or destroying their integrity.[2] All property, whether it is corporeal or incorporeal, is called ecclesiastical whenever it belongs to the universal Church, the Holy See or to some corporation in the Church.[3] Thus all church belongings are constituted as a class apart enjoying special immunities and safeguarded by special laws.[4]

Sacred and precious articles are not, strictly speaking, subdivisions of ecclesiastical goods, as they can at times be in the

---

[1] *Institutes* 2,2: "Corporales eae sunt, quae sui natura tangi possunt; veluti fundus. ... ... Incorporales autem sunt, quae tangi non possunt." *Digest* 8, 1, 14 pr. Ulpian, Reg., 19, 11.

[2] *Digest*, 7, 9, 1, 1; 19, 1, 40; 41, 1, 7, 10; 44, 7, 44, 1. Schmalzgrueber III, 1, 13. Reiffenstuel III, 13, 4. Ferraris v. *Alienatio* I, col. 367.

[3] D'Annibale III, n. 77.

[4] C. 13, X, *de verborum significatione*, V, 40. Conc. Trident., sess. XXII, *de ref.*, c. 11. S. C. C., *Calatageronen., Bonorum*, 25 Jan. 1902, *Thesaurus*, CLXI (1902) 60.

possession of laics.[1] Articles or objects destined for divine service are constituted sacred by consecration or benediction. In Roman law temples and altars consecrated to the gods were considered "res sacrae." Belonging to the deities they were considered "res divini iuris," and were consequently incapable of valuation, hypothecation, mortgage, usucapion or adaptation to any profane use.[2] In Canon law similar immunity from improper use is secured by consecration or benediction. Consecration is the more solemn form of blessing. Thus churches, altars, chalices, patens and the like are consecrated; while foundation stones, cemeteries, sacred vestments, images and church-bells are blessed.[3] For consecration at least episcopal power is necessary, unless special permission is granted in law or by apostolic indult.[4] On the other hand, except in a few instances, priests (and sometimes even deacons and lectors) may impart blessings.[5] The Church has always held the highest regard for objects thus consecrated or blessed. Canon 1150 exhorts that these be reverently handled; Canon 1537 expressly forbids their use in unbecoming circumstances or places. Canon 1539 prohibits any increase of price in the sale or exchange of sacred objects because of their blessing.[6]

Canon 1497, § 2, does not explicitly fix the value necessary to constitute an object precious, but merely states that it must be notable. The Church shows great wisdom in not determining an invariable rating, since with the change of times and generations money values tend to fluctuate; works of art have greater monetary appreciation in one period than another; each succeeding century tends to enhance the value of antiques, while numerous other factors may arise to increase or decrease the price of articles.

According to Canon 1497, § 2, objects are precious because of notable value due to their workmanship, such as paintings and statues;[7] by reason of their historical worth, such as autographs and manuscripts; and finally because of their inherent, intrinsic

---

[1] Canon 1510. Vermeersch-Creusen II, n. 819. Vogt, *Das kirchliche Vermögensrecht*, 54.

[2] Colquhoun §926. Sherman II, 559. Buckland 184.

[3] Phillips 423. Vogt 53.

[4] Canon 1147 §1.

[5] Canon 1147 §§§2, 3, 4.

[6] Vide etiam Canon 1306.

[7] Canon 1280; 1281 §1; 1497 §2.

worth, such as articles wrought in gold or jewels. Before the Code the term "precious" was further applied to fruit-bearing trees, flocks and herds from which incomes accrued to monasteries and churches.[1]

To be precious an object must be of notable value. Theologians and canonists are by no means in agreement as to the worth necessary to constitute this notable amount. This divergence of opinion is recognized in a recent decision of the S. Congregation of the Council where it is stated: "vix praetermittere oportet in determinatione notabilis valoris non parum discrepare ab invicem doctorum sententias."[2] Some authors go so far as to exclude even precious articles from the category of objects of notable value unless they are worth thirty thousand lire. Others, on the contrary, consider all precious articles to be of notable worth in the canonical sense, no matter what their monetary value might be.[3] These extreme views can hardly be accepted. Canons 534, § 1, and 1532, § 1, in making a distinction between precious articles and objects valued at more than thirty thousand lire clearly destroy the first contention; while the contrary opinions of many noted commentators weaken the probability of the second.[4] The common opinion in this matter before the Code was given by D'Annibale:—"Porro mobilia pretiosa accipimus vasa aurea vel argentea, gemmas, etc., et quae vel antiquitate praestant vel artificio, dummodo valeant saltem 25 aureis de Camera, idest libellas 235."[5] This amount was the accepted estimate in the Roman Curia for the seventeenth century.[6] Since that time, however, money values have fluctuated and now the purchase value of money is much less than then.[7]

For an object to be of notable value many authors believe that the value be about one thousand francs.[8] Pighi considers as

---

[1] Molina, *De iustitia et iure*, II, 465, n. 4. Ferraris v. *Alienatio*, I, col. 368. Schmalzgrueber III, 1, 13. Reiffenstuel III, 13, n. 16. D'Annibale III,78.

[2] 12 Jul. 1919, AAS, XI, 417.

[3] S. C. Conc., 12 Jul. 1919, AAS. XI, 417.

[4] Barbosa, *De officio et potestate episcopi*, III, alleg. 95, n. 39. Reiffenstuel III,13, 14. Ferraris v. *Alienatio*, I, 7. Schmalzgrueber III, 13, 27.

[5] *Summula Theologiae Moralis*, III, 77, nota 6.

[6] S. C. Concilii, 12 Julii 1919, AAS, XI, 417. Wernz III, 160, nota 140.

[7] Wernz III, 160, nota 140.

[8] Genicot-Salsmans II, 612. Raus, *Institutiones canonicae*, (Lugduni, 1924), 237. Bonnaert-Simeon, *Manuale iuris cononici*, (Gandae, 1924,), 989. Gury-Tummolo, *Compendium theològiae moralis*, (Neapoli, 1920) II, 969.

necessary a price that would much exceed one thousand lire.[1] Cerato,[2] with whom Cavigioli seems to agree,[3] considers a value of thirty thousand lire necessary to constitute an object of notable worth. Otherwise, he argues a person wishing to dispose of a piece of furniture worth one thousand lire would needs have recourse to the Holy See; whereas, if he wished to sell the house, which the piece of furniture adorns, worth nearly thirty thousand lire he could have recourse to the Ordinary. Chelodi,[4] likewise inclining to a liberal estimate, says that if in the seventeenth century a precious article was one valued at two hundred and twenty lire, then today we can well say twenty-two hundred lire. Vermeersch-Creusen object to the opinion that would[5] insist on a value of thirty thousand lire to constitute an object of notable worth but refrain from suggesting any specific amount.

The conclusion of the "votum" submitted to the S. Congregation of the Council was:—"Quare valor iste tutissime ad 750 lib. in Curia hodie definiri potest. Nec desunt, qui notabilem valorem infra 1000 lib. esse hodie negant; immo ipse can. 1532, § 2, dum alienationem distinguit rerum quae 1000 lib. attingunt et quae 1000 lib. superant, hanc aestimationem, quae simplicitate quoque commendatur, ratam habere videtur."[6]

On January 14, 1922,[7] the S. Congregation of the Council answered a series of questions regarding precious articles. In reference to one question, viz.:—"Utrum ad alienationem rerum utcumque pretiosarum, semper necessarium sit beneplacitum Apostolicum, an possit Ordinarius intra certae summae limites huiusmodi alienationem permittere," the reply was thus formulated:—"Ad Pontificiam Commissionem Codicis pro canonibus authentice interpretandis." In view of this it is possible that some definite ruling might be established by the Pontifical Commission. Such a reply, it is true, would settle many uncertainties and would insure the validity of transfers in which precious

---

[1] *Censurae latae sententiae et irregularitates*, 46.

[2] *Censurae vigentes ipso facto in C. I. C. excerptae*, 77.

[3] *De censuris latae sentatiae*, 143.

[4] *Ius poenale*, 89, nota 7.

[5] II, 819.

[6] S. C. C., *Dioecesis N*, *Donariorum Votivorum*, 12 Julii 1919, AAS. XI, 418.

[7] AAS, XIV, 160.

objects figure; but it seems highly improbable and hardly expedient that any definite sum will be determined in view of the difficulties mentioned above. If such a sum were fixed it might be in the neighborhood of one thousand lire; basing this conjecture on a recent decision of the Congregation of the Council.[1]

[1] AAS. XI, 416. Other norms to be kept in mind in such matters would be: Canons 534 §1; 727; 730; 1281 § 1; 1530; 1531; 1532. S.C.C., *Diocesis N*, 12 Julii 1919, AAS, XI, 416. S. C. C., *Lauden.*, 14 Jan. 1922, AAS. XIV, 160.

CHAPTER V.

Corporations Acquiring Church Property.

1. Tenure of Property Acquired by Church Corporations.

Canon 1499.

§ 1. Ecclesia acquirere bona temporalia potest omnibus iustis modis iuris sive naturalis sive positivi, quibus id aliis licet.

In Canon 1499, § 1, the Church states its right to acquire property by all the just means which the natural and positive law sanction for others. Every state recognizes the individual's right to own and acquire property.[1] Now the right of a corporation to acquire property is based fundamentally and ultimately on the same reasons that justify acquisition of property by an individual. Corporations and societies are groups of men whose individual rights are not destroyed when they associate for a common end. The Church as a perfect and necessary public society can justly claim and defend the exercise of the rights which societies and individuals enjoy. No state has the power to impugn this right of the Church. Ownership and property rights of ecclesiastical goods being rights of strict and commutative justice cannot be violated by any temporal sovereign, anymore than the rights of less important corporations.[2]

The most common means, besides purchase, recognized and employed by the Church in acquiring property are:—taxes, tributes, tithes, first-fruits, pious foundations, last wills, legacies, donations and prescription.[3] These are in strict accord with justice and are similar in many respects to the means whereby other corporations acquire property.

---

[1] Leo XIII, litt. encycl. *Quod apostolici*, 28 Dec. 1878, *Fontes* n. 576. Leo XIII, litt. encycl. *Immortale Dei*, 1 Nov. 1885, *Fontes* n. 592. Leo XIII, litt. encycl. *Rerum novarum*, 15 Maii 1891, *Fontes*, n. 611.

[2] Clemens XIII, const. *Alias ad Apostolatus*, 30 Jan. 1768 *Fontes*, n. 464.

[3] *Acta et Decreta Conc. Plen. Americae Latinae*, n. 826. Vogt 45.

§ 2. Dominium bonorum, sub suprema auctoritate Sedis Apostolicae, ad eam pertinet moralem personam, quae eadem bona legitime acquisiverit.

Canon 1499, § 2, declares that the ownership of temporal goods belongs, under the supreme control of the Apostolic See, to the juristic person that acquired these same goods legitimately. It is obvious from this statement that the proprietary rights of juristic persons in the Church are of primary consideration in Canon 1499, § 2. Acquisitive rights, then, are only of secondary importance here. However, in order to emphasize the interrelation of the two it seems necessary to outline the nature and the historical development of the idea of the specific corporations in which proprietary rights—and incidentally rights of acquisition—are vested, especially in the United States. For the sake of clearness and completeness a brief elucidation of the different concepts of juristic persons is subjoined. References to the various ecclesiastical corporations in the United States are made to give a clear idea of how and by whom temporal goods are acquired in this country. This is particularly important in matters of deeds, titles, last wills and bequests.[1]

Canon 1499, § 2, happily settles an age-old controversy. The older theologians and canonists held to the basic principles upon which the solution of the question of property rights depended, but their terminology was often inexact and variant. Thus Navarrus (Martin de Azpilcueta),[2] Donatus,[3] Azorus,[4] Suarez,[5] and Reiffenstuel[6] taught that God, Christ or a saint was the subject in whom ecclesiastical ownership was vested. Others, such as Tellez,[7] Cajetan[8] and Molina[9] considered ecclesiastical property to be under human dominion of either a particular church or the universal church to the exclusion of one another.

---

[1] For a fuller treatment of this subject the dissertation of Rev. Dr. C. J. Bartlett can be consulted with profit.

[2] *De reditibus ecclesiasticis*, II, 516.

[3] *Rerum regularium praxis resolutoria*, (Coloniae, 1675), I, 2, 14, q. 27, n. 1.

[4] *Institutiones morales*, II, 6, 1.

[5] *Opera*, XXIV, 443.

[6] III, 25.4.

[7] III, 13,2: "Dicendum est dominium rerum ecclesiasticarum residere penes ecclesiam illam particularem cui talia bona applicata sunt pro dote . . . Nec persona singularis habet dominium, sed sola communitas, persona autem singularis non ut talis sed ut pars et membrum communitatis habet in ipsis rebus ius utendi."

[8] 2, 2, quaest. 47, art. 1.

[9] *De iustitia et iure*, II, 30, 22.

Fagnanus[1] and Sanguineti[2] held that the Roman Pontiff was the sole owner of Church property; while Thomassin[3] considered ecclesiastical goods to be the property of the poor.

The Code in declaring that the ownership of property belongs to the moral person that acquired it under the supreme control of the Holy See, confirms the teaching of the Council of Trent,[4] the Provincial Council of New Granada which succinctly stated:—"Ad universae Ecclesiae caput spectat, altum rerum ecclesiasticatum dominium tueri et defendere sua bona eorumque administrationem moderari; at utile dominium et directum speciatim cuiusque singulorum ecclesiarum ad illam pertinet ecclesiam, cui tituli possessionis addicti sunt,"[5] and canonizes the opinions of eminent authors.[6] The wording of the Canon excludes the extreme views, inexactitudes and absurdities heretofore proposed. The corporation that acquires property enjoys the ownership of that property under the jurisdiction of the Holy See.[7]

Church property is usually incorporated in accordance with the civil laws of the country in which the property is held. This is done to insure stability, to safeguard property and to avert needless litigations. In this country there are several different methods under which Church property has been or can be held. From the earliest days of the Colonies church societies exercised some kind of corporate rights.[8] Gradually different methods of holding church property were evolved or recognized by law. At the present time methods most commonly known in the States are:—corporation sole, corporation aggregate and fee simple.

The form of ownership formerly commended for the Church in the United States was corporation sole.[9] This legal entity consists of one person at a time. When that person dies the fee is held in abeyance until a successor is elected. Upon his election to the office the successor assumes all the duties and privileges

---

[1] III, 7, 50.

[2] II, 7, n. 435.

[3] III, 3, cap. 26–33.

[4] Sess. XIV, *de ref.*, c. 9; Sess. XXV, *de regular.*, c. 3.

[5] *Coll. Lacensis*, VI, col. 554.

[6] Schmalzgrueber III, 25,2. Phillips 416. D'Annibale I, n. 43; III, n. 77. Laurentius 635. Wernz III, 139. Bargilliat n. 1484. Aichner, 819.

[7] III Conc. Plen. Balt. n. 264. Wernz III, n. 139.

[8] L. Johnston, *Religious Liberty in the United States*, *Catholic University Bulletin* IX, (1903), 61.

[9] III Conc. Plen. Balt. n. 267. P. A. Baart, *Catholic Fortnightly Review*, XIV, 4.

which the aims and ends of the established corporation direct.[1] This system of property ownership was resorted to by the dioceses of this country in an effort to liberate church property from the control of trustees, when the system of lay-trusteeism became a menace, as well as to concentrate the management of temporal affairs in the hands of bishops. This was a necessary precaution at a time when much property was being lost to the Church through insecure means of incorporation. In some States corporation sole was not recognized by law because the legislatures believed it was an undue privilege to the Church which was considered the principal beneficiary of such a law.[2] Most States, however, were more reasonable and allowed Church property to be held under the corporation sole system. Some States even went so far as to allow the creation of quasi-corporations sole without any express legislative authority;[3] while others authorized bishops to become corporations sole by fulfilling certain stipulated conditions, such as filing a statement, certificate or affidavit in order to give public notice of the existence of the corporation.[4]

Another means of holding Church property is by corporation aggregate, under which property is vested in a body corporate formed from a group of members of the society thus incorporated. The incorporators hold this property under their control, but their possession is the possession of the artificial person whose agents they are. They have a voice in the management of the property but this right is an authority and not an estate or title. They endeavor to further the work of the corporation they represent according to its aims and ends. In many respects their discretion is similar to the direction vested in the board of directors of any other corporation.[5]

---

[1] Weston v. Hunt, 2 Mass., 500. Brown v. Porter, 10 Mass. 93.

[2] Union Church v. Sanders, 1 Houst. (Del.), 100; 63 Am. Dec. 187.

[3] St. Antonio v. Odin, 15 Tex. 539. Santillan v. Moses, 1 Cal. 92. Beckwith v. St. Philip's Parish, 69 Ga. 564.

[4] Mora v. Murphy, 83 Cal. 12, 23 Pac. 63. Searle v. Roman Catholic Bishop of Springfield, 203 Mass. 493, 89 N.E., 809. Chiniquy v. Catholic Bishop of Chicago, 41 Ill. 148. Gump v. Sibley, 28 Atl. 977. A unique form of corporation sole, which has only indirect reference to this country, was originated by the Treaty of Paris concluding the Spanish-American War. In virtue of this treaty the Apostolic See is recognized by the United States Government as a corporation sole in the insular possessions ceded to this country by Spain. Art. VIII, cited in Ponce v. Roman Cath. Church, 210 U. S. 296, 310.

[5] North St. Louis Christian Church v. McGowan, 62 Mo., 279. People's Bank v. St. Anthony's Roman Cath. Church, 17 N. E., 408.

In 1911 the S. Congregation of the Council expressed its preference for this mode of incorporating ecclesiastical property in the United States.[1] The advantages of such a system, if recognized and protected by the laws of each State, are many. The rights of the clergy and the power of the bishop are in no wise jeopardized and at the same time the laity are represented. In some States, such as New York, Wisconsin, Minnesota and Michigan, five members are necessary to incorporate a parish. These are the bishop, the vicar general, the pastor and two laymen. The bishop, vicar general and the pastor remain trustees "ex-officio" and their successors take their places. The laymen are elected for specified terms. The bishop is constituted president, the vicar general and pastor as vice-presidents, the laymen as treasurer and secretary respectively. In case of dissolution of the corporation its property reverts to the bishop of the diocese. Thus the property is amply safeguarded from the dangers of the fee simple method because the death of a trustee does not affect the life of the corporation; from those of the trustee system, for the clergy retain the controlling power in the management of the property.

A third form of holding property is by fee simple in virtue of which a bishop holds and administers Church property in his own name by an absolute and full legal title. This form is resorted to only when the safer and more convenient methods are prohibited by State laws.[2] In this case the bishop is counselled to remember that although the full ownership of ecclesiastical property is given him by the civil law, nevertheless he is not the owner but only the administrator in the Church's estimation.[3] This form of property-holding proved so precarious that in 1840 the S. C. of Propaganda drew up regulations and suggestions for the safeguarding of ecclesiastical goods held in fee simple.[4] In 1911 the S. C. of the Council declared that this method of holding church property was to be abolished: "Methodus quam vocant *in Fee Simple* omnino est abolenda."[5]

---

[1] S. C. Conc., 29 Julii 1911, *Eccles. Review*, XLV, 1911, 585.

[2] II Conc. Plen. Balt. n. 204. III Conc. Plen. Balt. n. 267–268.

[3] C. 2, X, *de donationibus*, II, 24. III Conc. Plen. Balt. n. 267.

[4] S. C. de Prop. Fide, decr. 15 Dec. 1840, *Coll.* n. 916.

[5] *Periodica* VI, 101. *Eccles. Review* XLV, 1811, 585. As this declaration does not appear in the *Acta Apostolicae Sedis* it is subjoined here:

1. Ex methodis quae pro possidendis et administrandis ecclesiasticis bonis nunc vigent in Statibus Americae Foederatis ea ceteris praeferenda est, quae

Such a system had to be discarded for good reasons. Experience of half a century proved that it was not a feasible method for holding property under the laws of the United States. First, property held in fee simple was oftentimes subject to taxation in this country; secondly, in the event of bankruptcy the entire church property of a diocese could be assigned to the creditors; thirdly, the bishop was liable for all debts of the various parishes; fourthly, wills had to be made for the proper transfer of the church property and these could be broken or contested; fifthly, in the interim between the death of one bishop and the appointment of a successor everything was in utter confusion; sixthly, inheritance taxes were often exacted which meant an undue burden especially in the poorer dioceses; finally property willed to the bishop after his death could be claimed by the Church only with the greatest difficulty in many States.

2. Property of Divided or Extinct Corporations.

Canon 1500.

Diviso territorio personae moralis ecclesiasticae ita ut vel illius pars alii personae morali uniatur, vel distincta persona moralis pro parte dismembrata erigatur, etiam bona communia quae in commodum totius territorii erant destinata, et aes alienum quod pro toto territorio contractum fuerat, ab auctoritate ecclesiastica, cui divisio competat, cum debita proportione ex bono et aequo dividi debent, salvis piorum fundatorum seu oblatorum voluntatibus, iuribus legitime quaesitis, ac legibus peculiaribus, quibus persona moralis regatur.

As the Church grows and its different corporations flourish, it sometimes becomes expedient to divide a large ecclesiastical corporation so as to start another corporation of a similar nature. Parishes are usually divided in this way. A certain territory is

---

vulgo dicitur *Parish corporation*, cum illis tamen conditionibus et cautelis, quibus in statu Neo-eboracensi in usu est. Hanc igitur methodum Episcopi, si lex civilis consentiat, quoad bona temporalia in suam diocesim introducere statim curabunt. Si vero lex non consentiat, apud civiles auctoritates efficaciter instabunt ut quam primum concedatur.

2. In locis tantum in quibus a lege civili non admittitur *Parish Corporation* et donec eius concessio obtineri nequeat, permittitur alia methodus quae dici solet *Corporation sole*, ita tamen ut Episcopus in administratione bonorum ecclesiasticorum procedat, auditis interesse habentibus et consultoribus diocesanis, et in negotiis maioris momenti de eorum consensu, super hoc ipsius Episcopi conscientia onerata.

3. Methodus quam vocant in *Fee Simple* omnino est abolenda.

apportioned; the new parish is incorporated and funds are secured to begin the new undertaking.

The establishing of a new corporation or parish is often fraught with as many risks as a new business venture. Canon 1500 contemplates such difficulties and legislates on certain details in order to minimize the dangers by determining how and by whom the property involved will be acquired. After the division of territory has been made[1] it is the duty of competent ecclesiastical authorities to apportion the resources equitably.[2] In all cases the special circumstances, the acquired rights, the expressed intention of the founders and donors as well as the particular statutes must be observed, whether these emanated from the Holy See or other lawful superiors.[3]

Canon 1501.

Exstincta persona morali ecclesiastica, eius bona fiunt personae moralis ecclesiasticae immediate superioris, salvis semper fundatorum seu oblatorum voluntatibus, iuribus legitime quaesitis atque legibus peculiaribus quibus exstincta persona moralis regebatur.

Whenever an ecclesiastical corporation owning property becomes extinct this property is naturally acquired by some other juristic personality in the Church. Canon 1501 accordingly legislates for such cases. In virtue of Canon 102, § 1, an ecclesiastical corporation may become legally extinct in two general ways: by authorized suppression or by legal cessation after a hundred years of natural non-existence.

Since every subordinate corporation in the Church is a member of a higher juridical entity or at least of the universal Church it is but natural that temporalities of an extinct body should revert to the higher corporation.[4] The application of this principle is simple enough in regard to religious institutes which are hierarchically established.[5] But in the case of confraternities or independent monasteries the matter is far more difficult. It would seem that the diocese or the Holy See would then be the immediately higher juridical entity.[6] Furthermore, if such a

[1] Canon 216; 1423 §1; 1427 §3.
[2] Reg. 55 R.J. in VI°.
[3] Vermeersch II, 822.
[4] Canon 1501.
[5] Canon 493; 494 §2.
[6] Vermeersch-Creusen II, 822.

corporation were not suppressed the expiration of one hundred years would be necessary to render it canonically extinct.[1] In such a case it would seem that the temporalities of the moribund corporation are to be administered by the higher juridical body to which they are to be annexed at the expiration of the required time, unless some other ruling had been decided upon.[2]

---

[1] Canon 102 §1.

[2] Vermeersch-Creusen II, 822.

CHAPTER VI.

Contributions From the Faithful.

1. Tithes.

Canon 1502.

Ad decimarum et primitiarum solutionem quod attinet, peculiaria statuta ac laudabiles consuetudines in unaquaque regione serventur.

Tithes and first-fruits are among the oldest and best-known means by which the Church acquired temporal goods to carry on its work. Both were of strict precept among the Jews in virtue of Old Testament ordinances.[1] At an early age they were adopted by Christian communities as being easily adaptable to the needs of the Church and the incomes of the faithful.

Tithes, strictly speaking, constitute the tenth part of all the fruits and profits justly acquired due to God in recognition of His supreme dominion over men and paid to the ministers of His Church.[2] Such tithes are of three kinds: predial or those derived from the annual crops;[3] personal, those resulting from industry or occupation;[4] and mixed, which arise from things nourished by lands such as cattle, milk and wool.[5] Predial tithes were generally called greater tithes; while personal and mixed tithes were considered lesser tithes.[6]

---

[1] *Levit.* XXVII; *Deuter.* XIV, 22; *Malach.* III, 10. *Exod.* XXIII, 16, XXXIV, 22; *Deuter.* XXVI, 1-11.

[2] C. Paviensis (850), can. 17, *Ss. Conc.* XIV, 930. Wernz III, 211.

[3] S. Rom. Rot., *Ussellen., Decimarum super manutentione,* 28 Febr. 1689; *Decis. Nuperrimae S. Rom. Rotae,* Dec. 16, n.6, II, 19. Pallottini, v. *Decima,* VII, 77, n. 52–55.

[4] S. C. C., *Ausculana, Decimarum,* 20 Dec. 1873, *Thesaurus* CXXXII, (1873), 764. S. C. C., *Mutilana, Decimarum,* 5 Feb. 1876, *Thesaurus* CXXXV, (1876), 72. S. C. C., *Pisauren., Decimarum,* 28 Julii 1877, *Thesaurus* CXXXVI, (1877), 420.

[5] Barbosa, *Iuris Eccles. Universi,* III, 29, 5. Wex, *Manipulus Decimarum,* 5. Schmalzgrueber, III, 30, 5. Reiffenstuel III, 30, 3. Pirhing III, 30, §1,498. Ferraris, v. *Decimae,* I, 7.

[6] Reiffenstuel III, 30,5.

In the Didascalia[1] and the Apostolic Constitutions[2] tithes were mentioned as means of supporting the ministers of the Church and alleviating the wants of the needy. Following this doctrine writers of the Church stressed the obligation of the faithful to contribute. St. Irenaeus[3] and Origen[4] exhorted the people to give generously; St. Cyprian considered generosity in giving tithes as a true test of faith and a sure bond of union with the first Christians who sold their possessions to give to the poor,[5] and insisted that the faithful give tithes for the support of the Church so that day and night God's ministers could concern themselves only with spiritual matters.[6] Pope Damasus I declared that entrance to the churches was to be refused to those failing to pay tithes.[7] St. Augustine[8] emphasized the necessity of giving tithes as a means of overcoming pride and on another occasion declared that those who failed to give tithes were defrauding God who gave the blessings of rain and crops.[9] Caesar of Arles insisted that tithes were due because of God's bounty to the faithful and added a new reason that gained weight with the centuries, namely, that tithes had become strictly due in virtue of a universal custom.[10] At a later date St. Maximus of Tours re-affirmed the reasons adduced by St. Augustine and added that tithes were due from a mandate of God Himself.[11] St. Paulinus held that if the faithful were parsimonious toward God, His generosity would be measured to them in return;[12] and that tithes were to be paid because God so willed and in addition they were due from a universal custom of the Church.[13] St. Ivo, Bishop of Chartres, substantiated the Church's right to tithes by

---

[1] IX Nau, 52, *Dict. de Theolog.* II, col. 850.
[2] VII, 39, Funk, *Doctrina Duodecim Apostolorum*, 95.
[3] *Contra Haereses*, IV, c. 18, n. 2, MPG, VII, 1025.
[4] *Homilia XI in Numeros*, n.2, MPG, XII, 644.
[5] *De Unitate Ecclesiae*, c. 26, MPL, IV, 535.
[6] St. Cyprianus, *Epistola LXVI*, MPL, IV, 410.
[7] MPL, XIII, 1203.
[8] *In Psalm.* CXLVI, n. 17, MPL, XXXVII, 1911.
[9] Sermo CCLXXVI. MPL, XXXIX, 2264–2266. Vide etiam: Justinus Martyr, *Apologia*, n. 67, MPG, VI, 430. Tertullianus, *Apologia*, n. 39, MPL, I, 469. St. J. Chrysostomus, *Homilia LXIV*, MPG, LVIII, 615. St. Hieronymus, *In Malachiam III*, 7, MPL, XXV, 1568. Cassianus, *Collationes XXI*, cap. 3, MPL, XLIX, 1172.
[10] MPL, LXVII, 1078.
[11] *Sermo XXVI*, MPL, LXII, 901.
[12] *In Conc. Forojuliense* (796), Can. 14, MPL, XCIX, 32.
[13] *In Conc. Forojuliense*, Nota in Can. XIV, MPL, XCIX, 340.

quoting the rulings of the Councils.[1] So well-founded was the Church's right to tithes and so universal was the obligation that even civil rulers like Charlemagne[2] and William the Conqueror[3] sanctioned and protected these rights.

The teachings of the Fathers on tithes was gradually formulated into the laws of the Church. After the sixth century the legislation was definite and uniform,[4] viz., all the faithful were strictly bound to donate tithes for the support of the Church in God's honor; and those who failed in this duty were considered anathematized.[5] Because of the great emphasis placed upon the obligation of giving by the Fathers and the Councils some writers inferred that the strict proportion of one-tenth was due the Church by divine law.[6] Today, however, the generally accepted opinion is that ministers of Christ's Church are entitled to honest support by the natural and divine law; while it pertains to the ecclesiastical law to determine the exact proportion that the faithful are bound to contribute.[7]

The obligation of paying tithes devolved primarily and principally upon all baptized persons unless they were exempted by

---

[1] MPL, CLXI, 1093.

[2] *Benedicti Diaconi Capitulariorum Collectio*, MPL, XCVI, 725. *Francorum Regum Capitularia*, Can. III, Hludiwici Regis, MPL, CXXXVIII, 582.

[3] Lex. VII et VIII, MPL, CXLIX, 1334.

[4] The Second Council of Macon (585) stated that tithes were paid "longis temporibus," indicating that the custom existed long before definite laws were drawn up. C. Matisconensis II (585), can. 5, *Ss. Conc.* IX, 951.

[5] C. Turonensis (567), *Littera Synodalis*, *Ss. Conc.* IX, 808. C. Matisconensis II (585), can. 5, *Ss. Conc.* IX, 951. C. Rothomagense (649), can. 3, *Ss. Conc.* X, 1200. C. Calchutense (787), can. 17, *Ss. Conc.* XII, 947. C. Moguntiacum (813), can. 38, *Ss. Conc.* XIV, 73. Capitula Rodulfi Archiepiscopi Bituricensis, *Ss. Conc.* XIV, 953. C. Suessionense II (853), can. 9, *Ss. Conc.* XIV, 981. C. Rhemense II (813), can. 38, *Ss. Conc.* XIV, 81. C. Turonense III (813), can. 9, *Ss. Conc.* XIV, 85. C. Valentinum III (855), can. 10, *Ss. Conc.* XV, 9. C. Wormatiense (868), can. 59, *Ss. Conc.* XV, 879. C. Troslejanum (909), cap. IV–VI, *Ss. Conc.* XVIII[a], 273. C. Bundense (943), cap. II, *Ss. Conc.* XVIII[a], 399. C. Tolosanum (1119), can. 4, *Ss. Conc.* XXI, 227. C. Remense (1148), can. 8, *Ss. Conc.* XXI, 716. C. Cassiliense (1172), can.3, *Ss. Conc.* XXII, 134. C. Londoniense (1200), can. 9, *Ss. Conc.* XXII, 718. C. Burdegalense (1255), cap. XIII, *Ss. Conc.* XXIII, 861. C. Eboracense (1367), can. 5, *Ss. Conc.* XXVI, 465. C. Londoniense (1382), Conclusio VIII, *Ss. Conc.* XXVI, 696. C. 22, X, *de decimis, primitiis et oblationibus*, III, 30. Conc. Trident., sess. XXV, *de ref.*, c. 12. Martinus V, const. *Inter cunctas*, 22 Febr. 1418, *Fontes* n. 43.

[6] Fagnanus III, 32, 3. Hooker, *Antiquities of the Christian Church*, L. V, 5.

[7] St. Thomas 2, 2, q. 87, art. 1. Bellarminus, *De clericis*, I, c. 25. Wex 22. Laymann IV, 6, 2, n. 1. Reiffenstuel III, 30, 1, n. 7. Schmalzgrueber III, 30, 1, n.8–10. Ferraris, v. *Decimae*, I, n, 13–25. Devoti IV, I, 16, n.2. Wernz III, 214.

Apostolic indult, by legitimate custom, by compact or compromise.[1] By baptism the faithful became members of the Church subject to its obligations as well as its benefits. Infidels and Jews were not bound "per se" to pay tithes. However, if they owned property within the confines of parishes they could be held to the predial tithes.[2] In the early ages of the Church, before the dioceses were divided into parishes tithes were paid directly to the bishops. After this division they were paid to the pastor from whom the sacraments and other spiritual benisons were received.[3]

Predial tithes were offered immediately after the harvest;[4] while personal tithes were due at the end of the year.[5] Predial tithes were paid without any deduction for expenses or taxes; whereas these could be deducted from personal tithes.[6] Unless a special law or custom directed otherwise the donor of predial tithes fulfilled his obligations by leaving the prescribed portion of his crops in the fields and notifying the pastor or the tithe-collector of this fact.[7]

The custom of paying personal tithes has long ago fallen into desuetude;[8] but real tithes are still paid in varying forms in some countries.[9] The system of tithes was introduced into the United States by the early missionaries but it did not continue in force for long except in some localities. Canon 1502 supposes

---

[1] C. 16, X, *de decimis, primitiis et oblationibus,* III, 30. Reiffenstuel III, 30, 4, n. 60. Wernz III, 216.

[2] Schmalzgrueber III, 30, 1. Reiffenstuel III ,30, 3. Ferraris, v. *Decimae,* II, n. 35. Wernz III, 216.

[3] S. C. C., *Ariminen, Decimarum,* 8 Martii 1884, *Thesaurus* CXLIII, (1884), 252. DeLuca, *Theatrum veritatis et iustitiae,* III, 3, 6. Fagnanus, III, 5, 15–17. Schmalzgrueber III, 30, 1. Reiffenstuel III, 30, 5.

[4] Wex 122. Barbosa, *Iuris Eccles. Universi,* III, 26, 9. Thomassinus III, 1, 9, n.3.

[5] Wex 123. Schmalzgrueber III, 30, 2. Ferraris, v. *Decimae,* III, n. 18.

[6] C. un., *de decimis,* III, 7 in Extravagant. com. S. C. C., *Ausculana, Decimarum,* 14 Dec. 1872, *Thesaurus* CXXXI, (1872), 589. S. C. C., *Pisauren., Decimarum,* 28 Iulii 1877, *Thesaurus* CXXXVI, (1877), 420. Reiffenstuel III, 30, 1, n. 15.

[7] S. Rom. Rot., *Nicien., Decimarum,* 10 Dec. 1688, *Decis. Nuper. S. Rom. Rot.,* Decisio 207, n. 17, II, 272. S. Rom. Rot., *Nicien., Decimarum,* 23 Iunii 1690, *Decis Nuper. S. Rom. Rot.,* Decisio 90, n. 26, III, 123. Pallottini, v. *Decima,* VII, 73. Wex 120. Schmalzgrueber III, 30, 1, n. 17.

[8] Schmalzgrueber III, 30, 1, n. 12. Wernz III, 217.

[9] Conc. Prov. Quebec., III (1863), *Collectio Lacensis* III, 677. Tithes are still considered as a means of church support in several States of the Southwest where Spanish influence and customs remain.

the tithe system in vogue in some places and leaves existing conditions unchanged, commanding respect for particular laws and legitimate customs.

2. First-Fruits.

First-fruits hold a less prominent place in the history of Church goods than do tithes. Both forms were adopted as means of support in the early Church and were considered by the Fathers and Councils as concomitant parts of ecclesiastical revenue. Until the seventh century first-fruits continued to be mentioned almost inseparably with tithes. Gradually the two became clearly distinct. Tithes then received the greater attention and emphasis. After the thirteenth century first-fruits were rarely considered as important means of support. They fell into desuetude or were merged with tithes and other forms of offerings.[1]

The consecration of the first-fruits of the field to God was of strict precept for the Jews of the Old Covenant.[2] From the Old Testament they were introduced into the early Church and are mentioned in the Didache,[3] and the Apostolic Constitutions.[4] The Fathers and ecclesiastical writers refer frequently to first-fruits as a means of Church support.[5] Councils likewise make mention of the obligation of offering first-fruits.[6]

Since the Council of Trent the means of Church support have been better organized than formerly. The faithful have as a rule been exceedingly generous and hence the Church has not been forced to formulate detailed and stringent laws in order to secure means of existence. Canon 1502 allows great latitude to each district and country in this matter of church support. This exemplifies great wisdom on the part of the Legislator. With

[1] Pirhing III, 30, 9, 1.

[2] *Exodus* XXIII, 16; XXXIV, 22. *Deuteronomy* XXVI, 1-11. *Leviticus* XIX, 23-25; XXIII, 10-14.

[3] XIII, 3; Funk 41.

[4] VII, XXIX, Funk, 95.

[5] Origen, *Homilia XI in Numeros*, n. 2, MPG, XII, 644. St. Augustinus, *In Psalm. CXLVI*, n. 17, MPL, XXXVII, 1911. St. Maximus Taurinensis, *Sermo XXVI*, MPL, LVII, 901. St. Paulinus, *In Conc. Forojuliense* (796), MPL, XCIX, 302. Auctor Ignotus tempore Caroli Magni, MPL, CXXIX, 1261.

[6] C. Trullonis (692), can. 28, *Ss. Conc.* XI, 955. C. Aurelatense VI (813) can. 9, *Ss. Conc.* XIV, 60. C. Bundense (943), cap. II, *Ss. Conc.* XVIII^{a}, 399. C. Tolosanum (1119), can. 4, *Ss. Conc.* XXI, 227. C. Burdegalense (1255), cap. XIII, *Ss. Conc.* XXIII, 861.

the change of times and customs newer methods of securing temporalities prove more feasible than would an ill-adjusted and impracticable system of ages past.[1]

In this country different methods are employed to secure church funds. In their general lineaments they are modelled in some way on the pew-rent system which has been in vogue so long here.[2] The voluntary offerings of the faithful are generally sufficient to take care of the Church's needs; so that strictly defined laws have been unnecessary.

The question is often raised whether a person is to be refused the ministrations of the sacraments if he refuses to pay tithes or fails in his duty of church support. It may be stated that the general precept of contributing to the support of religion and its ministers is binding on all the faithful according to their means. Individual cases are to be judged according to the disposition of the person and the circumstances of the particular church and its members. The precept of church support binds gravely, but it is difficult to hold any individual delinquent guilty of grave sin unless his neglect to pay his just share should place the ecclesiastical ministers in dire need or impose an undue burden upon the other faithful.[3]

Kenrick maintains that if under the above mentioned circumstances a person persists in his refusal to contribute anything to the Church, he would be considered unworthy of sacramental absolution.[4] In this matter, however, it behooves all priests to be extremely circumspect. In answer to a question proposed from the diocese of Bardstown: "Licetne spirituale ministerium denegare iis, aut personis ad illorum spectantibus familiam, v.g. infantibus sacramentum Baptismi, si huic debito se submittere recusent," the S. Congregation of the Propaganda replied: "Indignam viro ecclesiastico, et animadversione dignam quaestionem de sacris et ipso Baptismate denegandis iis qui oblationum debito se submittere recusant."[5] The Third Plenary Council of Baltimore expressed a like counsel:—"Fama fert (quae utinam inanis mendaxque sit) nonnullis in locis inveniri sacerdotes qui, ubi gravis culpa non apparet, sacramentalis abso-

---

[1] Barbosa, *Juris Eccles. Universi*, III, 25, 7.

[2] Kenrick, Tract. IV, n. 64.

[3] S. C. de Prop. Fide, 13 Maii 1816, n. 3; *Coll.* n. 713. Genicot I, n. 434. Noldin II, n. 716. *Eccles. Review*, LXIX, 1923, 83.

[4] Kenrick, Tract, IV, n. 64.

[5] S. C. Prop. Fide, 13 Maii 1816, *Coll.* n. 713, 4.

lutionis beneficium denegant fidelibus, qui nolint collectis stipem dare, ad quam sub peccato gravi teneri non constet; imo etiam (quod longe detestabilius est) aegrotantibus ac morti proximis adsistere ac sacramenta praebere recusant. Vix animum inducere possumus, ut quidpiam tam atrox et indignum de ecclesiarum nostrarum ministris suspicemur. Si quis vero existat, qui tale quid attentaverit, memores sint Episcopi se muneri suo graviter deesse, nisi in reum pro merito animadvertant."[1] Hence pastors, in securing means for the support of their parishes, should take great care lest their appeals for revenue and offerings become unduly tinged with an avaricious desire to enrich their parishes. The faithful have a strict obligation to contribute to those causes that are intimately bound up with the support of God's ministers and His Church. This obligation, however, can hardly be stressed in drives for funds not essential for the Church's well-being.[2]

3. Alms Collecting.

Canon 1503.

Salvis praescriptis can. 621–624, vetantur privati tam clerici quam laici sine Sedis Apostolicae aut proprii Ordinarii et Ordinarii loci licentia, in scriptis data, stipem cogere pro quolibet pio aut ecclesiastico instituto vel fine.

The provisions of Canon 1503 will tend to obviate many abuses against which the Church has tried remedies for centuries.[3] Especially in this country have the faithful been imposed upon and the rights of pastors been interfered with by the indiscreet soliciting of alms. Missionaries from nearly all quarters of the globe have depended upon and at times have even exploited the generosity of American Catholics. Recognizing the harm that fund-collecting intruders could cause, the Third Plenary Council of Baltimore expressly forbade the soliciting of alms without the Ordinary's permission.[4]

---

[1] III Con. Plen. Balt. n. 292.

[2] S. C. C. *Nucerina et Marsorum, Decimarum,* 28 Jan. 1893, *Thesaurus,* CLII (1893), 65. S. C. de Prop. Fide, 1 Aprilis 1816, *Coll.* n. 712. III. Plen. Conc. Balt. n. 292–293. St. Thomas 2, 2, a. 87, art. 1. Laymann VI, 5, 4.

[3] C. 2, "*de poenitentiis et remissionibus,*" V, 9 in Clem. Conc. Trid., sess. XXI, *de ref.*, c. 9. S. C. C., *Albanen,* 28 Febr. 1723, Richter, 123. S. C. C.. *Pampilonen.*, 6 Maii 1741; Richter, 123.

[4] III Conc. Plen. Balt., n. 295. Vide etiam: Synodus Columbensis IV, (1902), 252. Synodus Dioecesana Denveriensis IV, (1904), Tit. VI, XLI.

The Canon under consideration here is directed against private persons whether clerics or laics; that is persons acting in private capacity. Pastors are not included in this prohibition as they act in their official capacity while exercising their rights within their own parishes.[1] Thus they are free to collect for their schools and other parish projects unless other restrictions are imposed by diocesan statutes or particular laws. Permission for private persons to collect alms can be obtained in two ways. The first is by permission of the Holy See, in which case the Sacred Congregation of the Council, the Sacred Congregation of Propaganda or the Sacred Congregation for the Oriental Church grants the rescript. Even when the collector has this Apostolic grant the local Ordinary can demand its presentation for recognition and verification.[2] The second method of obtaining permission to solicit funds is by securing the proper authorization from both the collector's own and the local Ordinary.[3] Strictly speaking the collector does not need authorization from the parish priests after he has secured this from the Ordinary, but courtesy would suggest and sometimes diocesan statutes demand that an understanding be reached with them.

A further restriction is that the collection be made for some pious or ecclesiastical purpose. This provision of the law is easily complied with as the faithful would be extremely reluctant to donate to a cause which was neither pious nor ecclesiastical in character. Another clause of the Canon to be noted is that the provisions of Canons 621–624 are to be observed. As Canon 624 intimates, the rulings of the decree of the Sacred Congregation of Religious of November 21, 1908, are to be followed.[4]

The Canon employs the phrase: "stipem cogere." Now collecting connotes soliciting help from a fairly large number of persons. Hence, it can be inferred that if a person were to ask aid of certain few acquaintances he would not be soliciting help in violation of the ruling of this Canon.[5] Likewise this pro-

---

[1] Canon 415 §2, 5°; Canon 630 §4.

[2] Canon 51. C. 2, *de poenitentiis et remissionibus*, V, 9 in Clem. Giraldus 888. Vermeersch, *Periodica*, IV, 307.

[3] S. C. Ep. et Reg., decr., 27 Martii 1896, *Coll.* n. 1924. S. C. de Religiosis, decr. 21 Nov. 1908, AAS I, 153. Ferraris, v. *Eleemosyna*, I, 36. Vermeersch, *De Religiosis et Institutis*, II, n. 200.

[4] AAS I, 153. It should be borne in mind that Franciscans or those deputed by them when taking up the collection for the Holy Land are not bound by the rulings of the Decree of 1908. AAS II, 729.

[5] Pruemmer, *Manuale Iuris Canonici*, 521.

hibition is considered to apply to personal collection tours, which are frequently indiscreet and importunate and so easily violate parochial rights and proprieties,[1] rather than to appeals for help by letter,[2] unless such appeals were made through notorious money-getting agencies employing means ill in accord with Christian charity and justice.

---

[1] Vermeersch-Creusen II, 823. Cocchi VI, 355.

[2] Augustine thinks otherwise: "The Code does not distinguish between personal or oral quest and begging by letters. Hence it includes both." *The Pastor According to the New Code of Canon Law*, 211.

CHAPTER VII.

CONTRIBUTIONS FROM CORPORATE GROUPS.

1. CATHEDRATICUM.

Canon 1504.

Omnes ecclesiae vel beneficia jurisdictioni Episcopi subiecta, itemque laicorum confraternitates, debent quotannis in signum subiectionis solvere Episcopo cathedraticum seu moderatam taxam determinandam ad normam can. 1507, § 1, nisi iam antiqua consuetudine fuerit determinata.

The cathedraticum is a moderate fee paid annually to a bishop as a token of deference and submission to the episcopal see.[1] It is called cathedraticum because it is given as a reminder that parish churches are sprung from the cathedral church;[2] and sometimes termed "synodaticum" when paid at the diocesan synod. It is also called "Paschalis," at times, when exacted after the Pasch.[3] Some older writers confused the term cathedraticum with the exaction that certain bishops made at ordination time, and which was more correctly called "pastellum" by Pope Gregory. This fee was rightly condemned as ill in accord with the laws of the Church.[4] In the first centuries custom rather than law suggested and regulated the payment of the cathedraticum.[5] Gradually laws were promulgated to insure on the one hand the payment of the tax, and on the other to curb any

---

[1] Benedictus XIV, *De Synodo Dioecesana*, Lib. V, cap. VI, n.2. Ferraris v. *Cathedraticum*, Art. I, n. 1. Santi III, 39, 6.

[2] S. C. C., *Aquilina*, *Cathedratici*, 24 Martii 1906; *Thesaurus*, CLXV (1906), 345. A. A. S. IX, 499. Fagnanus I, 16, n. 43. Ferraris, v. *Cathedraticum*, Art. I. n. 1.

[3] A. A. S. IX, 498. C. 16, X, *de officio judicis ordinarii*, I, 30. C. 20, X, *de censibus*, III, 39. S. C. C., *Caputaguen.*, *Subventionis*, 26 Junii 1702. *Decis Nuper. S. R. Rot.*, *Decis. 358, n. 5-7.* Benedictus XIV, *De Synodo Diocesana*, Lib. V, cap. 6, n. 2. Barbosa, *Juris Eccl. Universi*, III, 20, n. 1. De Angelis, *Praelectiones*, II, pars 2, 262. Sägmüller, 773.

[4] Gregorius Magnus, *In Synodo Romana*, Harduin III, col. 497. C. Bracarense III (572), can. 3, *Ss. Conc.* IX, 839. C. Trid., sess. XXI, *de ref.*, c. 1.

[5] Ferraris, v. *Cathedraticum*, Art. I, n. 5.

exorbitant exactions of bishops under this head. The earliest extant legislation on the matter is that of the Third Council of Braga which prescribed that the bishop could not exact more than two "solidi" from his churches for the cathedratic tribute:—"Placuit, ut nullus episcoporum, cum per dioeceses suas ambulant, praeter honorem cathedrae suae, id est, duos solidos, aliquid aliud per ecclesias tollat, neque tertiam partem ex quacumque oblatione populi in ecclesiis parochialibus requiret; sed illa tertia pars pro luminariis ecclesiae, vel recuperatione servetur, et singulis annis episcopo inde ratio fiat."[1] In later centuries Pope Gelasius urged that the cathedraticum be not extended beyond the customary amount;[2] Pope Pelagius designated the limit of this tribute as two "solidi";[3] Alexander III permitted bishops to exact the cathedraticum;[4] Innocent III sanctioned the same law;[5] and Honorius III obliged chapels and benefices to the payment of the cathedraticum.[6]

During the centuries preceeding the Council of Trent many bishops were considered reprehensible for their undue rigor, if not injustice, in exacting cathedratic tributes. Some were accused of exacting large amounts out of avarice; others of extorting fees from poor parishes that could ill afford any payments.[7] Thus St. Peter Damien intimated that many bishops looked upon the diocesan synod solely as an efficient means of collecting the synodaticum.[8] Such criticisms and aspersions continued for centuries; so much so, that some bishops such as St. Rudolph and Hincmar of Rheims abolished the "synodaticum" within their territories in order to remove themselves from all suspicion of avarice.[9]

After the Council of Trent some authors were of the opinion that the cathedraticum had been abrogated because bishops were not allowed to exact any fee while making their diocesan visita-

[1] C. Bracarense III, (572), can. 2, *Ss. Conc.* IX, 839. Similar legislation was enacted by the VII Council of Toledo, (646), can. 4, *Ss. Concilia*, X, 768., and the Council of Ravenna in 997, can. 2, *Ss. Concilia*, XIX, 219.

[2] C. 4, C. X, q. 3.

[3] C. 10, C. X. q. 3.

[4] C. 9, X. *de censibus, exactionibus et procurationibus*, II, 39.

[5] C. 20, X, *de censibus, exactionibus et procurationibus*, III, 39.

[6] C. 16, X, *de officio judicis ordinarii*, I, 31.

[7] Benedictus XIV, *Se Synodo Dioecesana*, V, 6, n. 4.

[8] *Opuscul.* 31, cap. 5; MPL, CXLV, 536.

[9] St. Petrus Damianus, *Opuscul. 31*, cap. 5; MPL, CXLV, 536. Hincmarus Rhemensis, *Capitula Archidiaconibus Presbyteris Data*, cap. V. MPL, CXXV, 801.

tions.[1] This opinion, however, did not long prevail as it was pointed out that the prohibition in no way extended to the cathedraticum, which was paid at stated times and had no direct relation with the episcopal visitation. Fagnanus and De Luca rightly maintained that it could never have been the Council's intent to abrogate so ancient, important and universal a tax without specific mention of the fact; for the cathedraticum was a right held by bishops in common law with a sanction of centuries behind it.[2] St. Charles Borromeo, an authoritative interpreter of the legislation of the Council of Trent, reenacted the law of the cathedraticum in his Second Synod of Milan, 1568, and this after the Council of Trent.[3] This authority, the resolutions and decisions of the Sacred Congregation of the Council and the uniform opinion of eminent canonists since the eighteenth century show conclusively that the cathedraticum was not abrogated by the Council of Trent.[4]

From the earliest times the amount of the cathedratic tribute was fixed as two "solidi,"[5] as is expressly mentioned in several

---

[1] Sess. XXIV, *de ref.*, c. 3.

[2] Fagnanus, I, 16, n. 43–60; III, 24, n. 16. De Luca, *Theatrum Veritatis et Justitiae*, VIII, 3, 38, n. 6.

[3] Since the decree of this Synod on the cathedraticum is of historical importance and is rarely found in collections, the text will be quoted in full here: "Illud sacris Canonibus constitutum est, ut a singulis parochis dioecesana Synodo cathedratici nomine solidi duo exigantur; idque argumento honoris, qui cathedrali Ecclesiae tanquam matri a caeteris parochialibus Ecclesiis tribui debetur nos tamen hanc pecuniae summulam, quae superioribus temporibus huic Metropolitanae Ecclesiae eo nomine debita est, nec persoluta tamen, eam omnem etsi iure nostro exigere poteramus, quoniam quod eo nomine solui debet praescribi non potest, remittimus ac condonamus iis ipsis parochis, qui hoc ipsum cathedraticum praestare debebant. Sed ut in omni re Metropolitanae nostrae Ecclesiae dignitatem et ius retineamus, et quantum in nobis est, conservemus; illud universos et singulos parochos monemus, ut reliquis quae Deo dante in posterum quotannis habentur Synodis dioecesanis, hos ipsos duos solidos, quos honoris erga se Metropolitanae Ecclesiae iure debere sciunt, omnino persolvant."

Decretum XLI, *Acta Eccles. Mediol.*, p. 364. Vide etiam: S. C. C., *Civitatis Castelli et Alatrina*, 20 Aug. 1917, AAS IX, 499. *Acta Conc. Bituricensis* (1584) Tit. 33, can. 7, Harduin X, col. 1492. Benedictus XIV, *De Synoda Dioecesana*, V, cap. 6, n. 5.

[4] S. C. C., *Albinganen*, 2 Dec. 1644, Richter 336. S. C. C., *Amalphitana*, 5 Sept. 1705, Richter 336. S. C. C., *Civitatis Castelli et Alatrina*, 20 Aug., 1917, AAS IX, 500. Thomassinus III, 2, cap. 34. Wernz III, 223.

[5] Equivalent to about sixty cents according to present day computations. Ayrinhac, *Constitution of the Church in New Code of Canon Law*, 175.

[6] C. Bracarense III (572), can. 2, *Ss. Conc.* IX, 839. C. Toletanum VII (646), can. 4, *Ss. Conc.* X, 768.

councils;[6] and uniformly insisted on in later legislation.[1] This tax is purposely kept low in order to make manifest the Church's intention that the cathedraticum be given as a token of honor and subjection to the bishop rather than as a means of support proportionate to the wealth and size of parishes. This point was insisted on in a recent decision of the Congregation of the Council.[2] Some bishops of France had proposed a new plan for the introduction of the cathedraticum into their dioceses. They suggested a tax to be levied upon confraternities and parishes in proportion to the number of members. To this the Congregation objected because in virtue of such a plan the amount paid would exceed the limits of moderation prescribed by law and tradition in the Church and secondly such a system would destroy the essentially honorific character of the cathedraticum and make it a purely fiscal exaction ill in accord with the ancient canonical concept of this tribute.[3]

The Code does not determine the exact amount of the cathedraticum but leaves this to the provincial councils or a meeting of bishops, unless the amount has been determined by custom of long standing. In the determining of this sum the nature of the cathedraticum as merely a "signum recognitionis honoris" is not to be lost sight of.[4]

The cathedraticum becomes due to a bishop from the day on which he takes possession of his see.[5] A cognate question arises here whether any cathedraticum is to be paid to the Vicar Capitular or the Administrator. In the legislation of Honorius III it is stated that the cathedraticum is due to the bishop,[6] but there is no mention whether this tribute is to be paid to the Vicar Capitular or Administrator, whether it is due at all from the different parishes while the episcopal see is vacant, and if due whether it is reserved for the new bishop.

From the nature and scope of the tax as understood in later legislation it is evident that the cathedraticum or synodaticum

[1] C. 4, 8, 10, C.X, q.3. C. 16, X, *de officio iudicis ordinarii*, I, 31. Synodus Romana (1725) Tit. VIII, cap. 4:—"Cathedraticum a clerici debeautcr, quod est duorum solidorum, viginti scilicet iuliorum, censum Cathedrali Ecclesiae solvendi," etc. *Collectio Lacensis* I, 358.

[2] S. C. C., *Dioecesis N. et Aliarum in Gallia*, 13 Martii 1920, AAS XII, 446.

[3] S. C. C., *Dioecesis N. et Aliarum in Gallia*, 13 Martii 1920, AAS XII, 446.

[4] AAS XII, 445.

[5] Canon 349 §2. S. C. C., *Amalphitana, Cathedratici*, 5 Nov. 1707; Richter 335. S. C. C., *Carnerinen., Cathedratici*, 18 Martii et Julii 1725; Richter 335. S. C. C., *Anglonen et Tursien., Jurium*, 31 Jul. 1852; *Thesaurus*, CXI, 318.

[6] C. 16, X, *de officio judicis ordinarii*, I, 31.

was not given on account of the synod, but rather the synod was merely the occasion for the paying of the tax to the bishop as a sign of subjection. Even if no synod took place the tribute had to be paid.[1] Furthermore it is the bishop who is the "verus sponsus Ecclesiae suae, per matrimonium quoddam spirituale, quod cum ea iniit, et proprius pastor gregis subi commissi." This is an additional reason why the tribute should be paid to him alone, to the exclusion of every one else. A Vicar Capitular or Administrator is not a true shepherd of the flock, but a mere protector awaiting the real shepherd.[2] The conclusion then is that "vacante sede episcopali, Cathedraticum non debetur." This is borne out by a recent decision of the Sacred Congregation of the Council which is in accord with the decisions of the past centuries.[3]

According to Canon 1504 the cathedraticum is due from all churches under episcopal jurisdiction. This includes parish and collegiate churches; public secular oratories; likewise churches and parishes attended by religious.[4] The payment of the cathedraticum is obligatory for all benefices[5] under the bishop's jurisdiction. Therefore it is due from all pastors[6] and those canons who enjoy an individual prebend. If a group of canons were supported from one common stock, then only one cathedratic tribute would be exacted and this from the common fund.[7]

[1] C. 20, X, *de censibus, exactionibus et procurationibus*, III, 39. Benedictus XIV, *De Synoda Dioecesana.*, V, 8, n. 7.

[2] Canon 441, 2°; 430§ 3, 3°; 194§ 2. S. C°. C., *Civitat's Castelli st Alatrina*, 29 Aug. 1717, AAS. IX, 499.

[3] A. A. S., IX, 500. S. C. C., *Januen, Emolumentorum*, 23 Feb. 1856; *Thesaurus*, CXV, 76. S. C. C., *Anglonen et Tursien.*, *Jurium*, 31 Jul. 1852; *Thesaurus*, CXI, 318. Richter, *Canon et Decr. C. Trid.*, 336. Benedictus XIV, *De Syn. Dioec.*, Lib. V, cap. VIII, n. 7. Cocchi VI, 357.

[4] AAS, XII, 445. S. C. C., *Aquilina, Cathedratici*, 24 Martii 1906, *Thesaurus*, CLXV (1906), 345. Fagnanus I, 16, n. 43.

[5] Canon 1409–1415.

[6] It is evident from the letter of the Apostolic Delegate to the Bishops of the United States, Nov. 10, 1922, that all parishes in the United States having a resident pastor, an endowment or sufficient resources and defined boundaries are benefices; and the pastors have all the obligations of canonical pastors.

Ayrinhac, *Constitution of the Church in the New Code of Canon Law*, 25. Augustine, *The Canonical and Civil Status of Catholic Parishes in the United States*, 63.

[7] Conc. Romanum (1725), Tit. VIII, cap. 4, *Collectio Lacensis*, I, 358. III Prov. Conc. Westmonasterii (1859), Decr. XVII, Tit. 2, *Coll. Lacensis* III, 1022. *Acta Plen. Conc. Latinae Americae* n. 860.

Benedict XIV held that all pastors, irrespective of their Rite, were obliged to the cathedraticum as long as they resided in the diocese and were under the jurisdiction of the bishop. This opinion was based on a decision of the Sacred Congregation of the Council, 8 Feb. 1738, *Thesaurus*, VIII, 23.

Finally, the cathedraticum is due from lay confraternities[1] provided they have their own church. Hence they would not be bound to this tax if they possessed only a chapel, or an altar in a church.[2]

2. The Charitable Subsidy.

Canon 1505.

Loci Ordinarius, praeter tributum pro Seminario, de quo in can. 1355, 1356, aut beneficialem pensionem de qua in can. 1429, potest, speciali dioecesis necessitate impellente, omnibus beneficiariis, sive saecularibus sive religiosis, extraordinariam et moderatam exactionem imponere.

In Canons 1496, 1502–1504 the Code emphasizes the obligations of church support incumbent directly or indirectly upon the faithful. It is well then that Canon 1505 should define certain limitations to the Ordinary's power of imposing taxes and fees so that indiscreet zeal and avarice might never burden the faithful.[3] Unrestricted rights of bishops to exact any number of taxes and collections would work as much havoc in the ecclesiastical regimen as would the other extreme, viz., the unqualified refusal of the faithful to support the Church. Canon 1505 substantially restates the legislation of the Third Lateran Council (1179)[4] and that of Honorius III (1216–1227) to the Bishop of Assisi.[5]

The "Ordinarius loci"[6] is the person authorized to exact the charitable subsidy. Hence Vicars General are not expressly excluded by the Canon from exercising this right. In the old law the nature of the matter and the opinions of the older commentators seemed to deny them this power unless they had a special

[1] Can. 707 § 2; Can. 708.

[2] S. C. C. *Firmana*, 24 Julii 1734; Richter 336. S. C. C. *Urberetana*, 20 Martii 1745; Richter 336. Benedictus XIV, *De Synoda Dioecesana*, cap. 7, n. 4. *Il Monitore Eccles*, (1911). XXXVI, 366.

[3] C. 6, *de censibus, exactionibus et procurationibus*, III, 39. C. 2, *de censibus, exactionibus et procurationibus*, III, 20 in VI. C. un., *de censibus, exactionibus et procurationibus*, III in Extravag. com.

Many authors have quoted Gratian, C. 7, C. X, q. 3, as a source for the charitable subsidy. This, however, can constitute no authoritative reference as is clear from the text in Mansi, *Ss. Conc.* XIV, 95: C. Cabilonense II, (813), Can. 6: "Ecclesia vero sancta non solum fideles spoliare non debet: quia potius inopibus opem ferre, ut debiles, pauperes, viduae, orphani et ceteri necessitatem patientes, a sancta ecclesia, ut puta matre et omnium gubernatrice, *subsidium accipiant.*"

[4] C. 6, X, *de censibus, exactionibus et procurationibus*, III, 39.

[5] C. 16, X, *de officio iudicis ordinarii*, I, 31.

[6] C. 198 §2.

mandate from the Bishop.[1] The Canon does not expressly mention the necessity of advice from the diocesan chapter or consultors before levying such a tax, but in a matter of such importance it would be politic for the Ordinary to seek counsel.[2] The subsidy may be levied whenever a special diocesan need requires it. The older legislation of the Third Lateran Council and Honorius III required the existence of manifest and reasonable causes, evidently allowing greater latitude than the present law. Commentators generally considered sufficient reasons for imposing the subsidy to be:—expenses incurred in the consecration of a bishop, necessary and extraordinary repairs of the cathedral church, unusual diocesan debts, expenses of the "ad limina" visits of the bishop or his journey to a council. These reasons held only in those cases where the episcopal funds were insufficient to defray the expenses.[3]

Those obliged to the payment of the charitable subsidy are all beneficiaries, whether secular or religious. This is in accordance with the old law.[4] Exempt religious are not bound by this obligation.[5] The amount of the subsidy is not specifically determined in law. It should be moderate;[6] and although it can be resorted to occasionally it should nevertheless remain an extraordinary means.[7]

---

[1] Reiffenstuel, III, 39, 1, n. 22. Ferraris, v. *Subsidium Caritativum*, n. 12. Schmalzgrueber III, 39, n. 58. Barbosa, *Juris Eccles. Universi*, 21, n. 21.

[2] Conc. Plen. Amer. Latinae, n. 861. Pruemmer, 522. S. C. C. *Gerunden*.. 17 Feb. 1663, 26 Jan. 1760. Giraldus 397. Pallottini, v. *Episcopus*, XVIII. Reiffenstuel III, 39, 2, n. 34. Ferraris, v. *Subsidium Caritativum*, n. 16, Zallinger III, 39, 445 maintained that the bishop should have the consent or at least the advice of his chapter in deciding the need of a subsidy of charity. Joann. Andrea III, 39, n. 7. Barbosa, *De officio et potestate Episcopi*, Alleg. 87, n. 26.

[3] S. C. C. *Gerunden*, 17 Feb. 1663; 26 Jan. 1760, Richter, 337. S. C. C. *Caputaguen*, *Subventionis*, 26 Junii 1702, *Decis. Nuperrimae S. Rom. Rotae*, Decis, 358, n. 3, VII, 613. Barbosa, *De officio et potestate episcopi*, Alleg. 87, n. 29–35. Barbosa, *Juris ecclesiae universae*, III, 21 n.22–30. Fagnanus III, 16, n. 38. Pirhing III, 39, 4. Schmalzgrueber III, 39, 60. Reiffenstuel III, 39, 2, n. 30.

[4] Barbosa, *De officio episcopi*, Alleg. 87, n. 39. Schmalzgrueber III, 39, 4, n. 62. Reiffenstuel III, 39, II, n. 24. Ferraris, v. *Subsidium caritativum*, n. 29.

[5] S. C. C. 18 Feb. 11, Martii 1713, *Thesaurus* IX, 224. Schmalzgrueber, III 39, 4, n. 65. Ferraris, v. *Subsidium caritativum*, n. 46.

[6] Barbosa, *De officio et potestate episcopi*, Alleg. 87, n. 37. Reiffenstuel III, 39, 2, n. 32. Ferraris, v. *Subsidium caritativum*, n. 25.

[7] In Italy after the time of Innocent XI a bishop could levy the subsidy of charity only at the time of his accession to his see. The amount could be no greater than that exacted within the forty years previous. Innocentius XI, Const. 43, 10; *Bullarium*, VIII, 61. S. C. C. *Algaren*, *Subsidii caritativi*, 5 Jul. 1738, Giraldus, p. 396. Giraldus, *Expositio juris pontificii*, Sect. 583, p. 397

3. Restriction of Ordinary Tributes.

Canon 1506.

Aliud tributum in bonum dioecesis vel pro patrono imponere ecclesiis, beneficiis aliisque institutis ecclesiasticis, quanquam sibi subiectis, Ordinarius potest tantummodo in actu fundationis vel consecrationis; sed nullum imponi tributum potest super eleemosynis Missarum sive manualium sive fundatarum.

From the time of the Council of Chalcedon[1] the rights of bishops to ordinary taxes and pensions have been recognized by law. These were generally known under the term of ancient taxes and although considered in some respects similar to the cathedraticum, were viewed primarily as means of church support.[2] As was to be expected the exactions of bishops in virtue of this right were generally moderate and in proportion to the income of the parishes. Hence there was little or no need of further legislation on the matter. But during the unsettled times of the eleventh and twelfth centuries, when struggles between popes and kings, bishops and princes were frequent, the taxes imposed by the bishops became so numerous and inequitable that stringent legislation was necessary to restrict the number and amounts of fees levied upon churches and benefices. The Third Lateran Council (1179) adopted the first restrictive measures with universal sanction:—"Prohibemus insuper, ne ab abbatibus, vel episcopis vel aliis praelatis novi census imponantur ecclesiis, nec veteres augeantur, nec partem redituum suis usibus appropriare praesumant; sed libertatem, quam sibi maiores conservare desiderant, minoribus quoque suis bona voluntate conservent. Si quis vero aliter fecerit, irritum quod egerit habeatur."[3] Despite this severe legislation Lucius III (1181-1185),[4] Clement III (1187–1191)[5] and Clement V (1305–1314)[6] were constrained to repeat similar prohibitions, so deep-rooted and persistent had abuses become.

Canon 1506 is similar in many respects to the older legis-

---

[1] C. Chalcedonensis (451), Act. X, *Ss. Conc.* VII, 270.

[2] Zallinger III, 39, 445.

[3] C. 7, X, *de censibus, exactionibus et procurationibus*, III, 39. C. Londonense (1200), c. 8. *Ss. Conc.* XXII, 717.

[4] C. 23, X, *de jure patronatus*, III, 38. C. 13, X, *de censibus exactionibus et procurationibus*, III, 39.

[5] C. 15, 2, *de censibus, exactionibus et procurationibus*, III, 39.

[6] C. un. *de excessibus praelatorum*, V, 6, in Clem.

lation. The latter forbade the imposing of new taxes or the increasing of the previous ones;[1] while the Code permits the Ordinary to impose this additional tax on churches, benefices and ecclesiastical institutes upon only two occasions. These times are: on the occasion of the approval of the tablets of foundation,[2] or at the consecration, according to Canon 1155, which excludes the Vicar General from performing this function and consequently from levying the tax unless he has a special mandate.[3]

4. Determination of Fees in a Province.

Canon 1507.

§ 1. Salvo praescripto can. 1056 et can. 1234, praefinire taxas pro variis actibus iurisdictionis voluntariae vel pro exsecutione rescriptorum Sedis Apostolicae vel occasione ministrationis Sacramentorum vel Sacramentalium, in tota ecclesiastica provincia solvendas, est Concilii provincialis aut conventus Episcoporum provinciae; sed nulla vi praefinitio eiusmodi pollet, nisi prius a Sede Apostolica approbata fuerit.

From the first centuries the Church took great care lest any species of simony might insinuate itself in the sacramental system. There was always the lurking danger that offerings made on the occasion of the administration and reception of the sacraments might be considered as their price instead of being viewed as a contribution for the support of the clergy or a recompense for extraordinary labor. Some of the earlier councils forbade the faithful to make any offering upon the occasion of the administration of the sacraments lest the ministers would appear to sell holy things. Later on the clergy were forbidden to exact any fee for the administration of the sacraments, but devout Christians usually made a free-will offering; while those who neglected to do so were not infrequently reminded of the existing customs. In the Fourth Lateran Council (1215), Pope Innocent III[4] declared that the sacraments ought to be administered freely, but that the faithful ought to conform to the praiseworthy and long-established custom of making an offering on that occasion;

[1] Schmalzgrueber III, 39, I, n. 10. Reiffenstuel III, 39, I, n. 7–8. Pirhing III, 39, II.

[2] Schmalzgrueber III, 39, I, n. 10. Reiffenstuel III, 39, I, n. 7.

[3] Schmalzgrueber III, 39, I, n. 10. Reiffenstuel III, 39, I, n. 7.

[4] C. 42, X, *De simonia et ne aliquid pro spiritualibus exigatur vel promittatur*, V, 3.

and that bishops should when necessary compel them to do so. With this concession granted in law it became necessary to define the limits of all offerings and exactions as well as to correct abuses that crept in from time to time.

The first systematized, complete and satisfactory church laws on chancery and other fees were formulated by Innocent XI, Oct. 8, 1678.[1] The intention of this Pontiff was to have a uniform rate regulating the charges for the various acts, instruments or writings expedited from chanceries, and at the same time to put an end to the seemingly interminable disputes about exorbitant taxes.[2]

Pre-Tridentine legislation in this matter consisted mainly of conciliar enactments that lacked uniformity and clearness.[3] The Council of Trent[4] prohibited the exaction of fees and even the acceptance of offerings in connection with the conferring of Holy Orders; but allowed notaries to receive a tenth of a golden crown for expediting dimissorials and testimonial letters—provided no contrary custom prevailed—if no salary had been assigned to them for the discharge of their office and provided further, that no emoluments would accrue directly or indirectly to the bishop.[5] This legislation proved effective within its own scope, but was neither specific nor extensive enough to take care of all exigencies and cases.

The laws of Innocent XI forbade bishops, their vicars general and other officials to ask or accept anything in relation to the conferring of Orders or for any acts or documents pertaining to ordination, for appointments to parishes or benefices; for dispensations from matrimonial impediments, proclamation of banns and the like; for admission of nuns to profession; for the administration of the sacraments of baptism, confirmation, penance, eucharist, and extreme unction; for special blessings; for the approbation and publication of indulgences and for the

---

[1] *Bullarium Innocentii XI*, VIII, 61. Ferraris v. *Taxa*, n. 1.

[2] S. C. C., 10 Junii 1896, *Coll.* n. 1939.

[3] C. Toletanum (675), can. 8, *Ss. Conc.* XI, 142. C. Ravennatense (997), can. 1, *Ss. Conc.* XIX, 219. C. Bituricense (1031), can. 12, *Ss. Conc.* XIX, 504. C. Tolosanum (1056). can. 1, *Ss. Conc.* XIX, 847. C. Londonense (1200), can. 8, *Ss. Conc.* XXII, 717.

[4] Sess. XXI, *de ref.*, c. 1.

[5] By way of exception the bishop was allowed to receive the candle proffered to him by the person being ordained. Gasparri, *De sacra ordinatione*, n. 1121.

execution of briefs of the Sacred Penitentiary.[1] In conformity with the concession of the Council of Trent the decree of Innocent XI allowed chancellors a moderate recompense for their labor in drawing up requisite papers and documents.[2] The law of Innocent XI was intended primarily for Italy, but was considered a safe norm for the dioceses outside of Italy.[3]

On June 10, 1896, the Congregation of the Council issued a decree stating principles to direct bishops in determining the fees to be exacted or accepted in their dioceses. The imposition of fees in accordance with the rules of prudence and justice in sacramental matters was permitted provided that the sacraments were conferred freely, that pious customs were observed and all taint of simony carefully removed. As regards other acts not directly concerning the administration of sacraments such as dispensations from the proclamation of banns and the conferring of baptism in private homes certain considerations were to be observed, viz: laudable customs were to be observed and prudent consideration given to times, places and persons; the truly poor were to be exempt from all taxes; the fees were not so great as to deter anyone from the reception of the sacraments; all matrimonial fees were to be waived if there was any danger of concubinage; the taxes of benefices were to be proportioned to the incomes. It was further decreed that the taxes and fees were to be determined by provincial synods or the meetings of the bishops of a province and that the rates agreed upon were to be transmitted to the Congregation of the Council for ratification.[4]

With the former legislation as a background the aim and scope of Canon 1507, § 1, can be easily discerned. Provided the rulings of Canons 1056 and 1234 are observed fees can be stipulated for the various acts of voluntary jurisdiction; for the execution of papal rescripts[5] or upon the occasion of the ministra-

---

[1] S. C. C., *Amalphitana,* 18 Jul. 1699, Richter 334. S. C. C., *Policastren.*, 28 Sept. 1743, Richter 335. S. C. C., *Amerina.*, 22 Dec. 1755, Richter 335. S. C. C., *Ferentina.*, 20 Apr. 1782, Richter 335.

[2] Craisson, n. 1053.

[3] S. C. C., *Vasionensi,* 6 Febr. 1734, Richter 335. S. C. C., *Alexanensi,* 1 Sept. 1742, Richter 335. S. C. C., 10 Junii 1896, *Coll.* n. 1939.

Some authors—Bouix, *De episcopo,* II, 313; Ferraris, v. *Taxa,* n. 12, VII, 803, believed the observance of the decree of Innocent XI was obligatory outside of Italy and its adjacent insular dioceses, but the decree of the Cong. of the Council of 1896 states that the contrary was the common opinion.

[4] *Coll.* n. 1939 A.S.S. XXIX, 433.

[5] Canon 51; 54, §1, §2; 201. Thomassinus III, 1, 68.

tion of sacraments and sacramentals. In all these cases every danger of simony of the divine and ecclesiastical law is to be avoided,[1] and the truly poor are never to be discriminated against. When the bishops in provincial councils or informal meetings determine the fees for their provinces they must be guided not only by the needs and customs of their province, but also by the rulings of the decree of Innocent XI as well as that of the Congregation of the Council of June 10, 1896. A recent decision of the Congregation of the Council shows the necessity of adhering to the lineaments of the older legislation.[2] The list of the rates determined upon by the bishops is to be transmitted for the approval of the Holy See, which in this case would be the Congregation of the Council.[3] Until this schedule of taxes is approved it remains ineffective.

In the matter of the execution of papal rescripts it should be borne in mind, especially in this country, that the diocesan fee is to be less than the pontifical tax according to a ruling of the Normae: "In omni rescripto, indulto, dispensatione a suo Officio indicabitur . . . etiam pecuniae summa, cuius repetendae ius habet diocesana Curia pro exsecutione rescriptorum, si haec necessaria sit; quae quidem summa pontificia taxatione erit inferior."[4]

When granting matrimonial dispensations bishops and diocesan officials are forbidden in virtue of Canon 1056 to exact any fee except a small offering to defray chancery expenses,[5] unless they have express permission of the Holy See to exact more. If they make exactions contrary to the rulings of Canon 1056 they are bound to restitution. Likewise if pastors exact larger fees than allowed by lawful custom or diocesan regulations they are bound to restitution in virtue of Canon 463, § 2.[6]

The determination of diocesan and provincial fees in accordance with Canon 1507, § 1, and the other regulations of the Canon itself have a very important bearing upon matters of

---

[1] Can. 730.

[2] S. C. C., *Dioceses N. et Aliarum*, *Taxarum Curiae*, A.A.S. XIII, 350.

[3] Can. 250 §2. S. C. Consist., 21 Apr. 1910, A.A.S. II, 330.

[4] *Ordo. serv. in R. Curia*, I, *Norm. Comm.*, cap. XI, A. A. S. I, 55, n. 2.

[5] Conc. Trident., sess. XXIV, *de ref. matrim.*, c. 5. Clemens XIV, ep. encycl. *Decet quam maxime*, 21 Sept., 1769, 17–19, *Fontes*, n. 467. S. C. de Prop. Fide, instr., 8 Sept. 1869, n. 52; *Coll.* n. 1346.

[6] Funeral fees and offerings are regulated and determined by the Ordinaries with the advice of their cathedral chapters or diocesan consultors. Canon 1234 §1. C. Ravennatense (997), c. 3, *Ss. Conc.* XIX, 219. C. Bituricense (1031), c. 12, *Ss. Conc.* XIX, 504.

parochial and diocesan administration. Canon 463 enunciates the pastor's right to offerings and fees authorized in accordance with Canon 1507, § 1, together with the obligation of restitution if more is exacted; Canon 736 strictly limits the ministers of the sacraments to the offerings authorized by Canon 1507, § 1; while Canon 2408 states the punishments for those who increase or exact fees without proper authorization.

This Canon, extensive in scope, is obviously an important norm in regulating points of law and discipline of frequent occurrence. The proper observance of this Canon, both in letter and in spirit, will obviate discord and difficulties; will safeguard the interests of the Church and its ministers, and happily avert dangers of simony.

Canon 1507.

§ 2. Ad taxas pro actibus iudicialibus quod spectat, servetur praescriptum can. 1909.

The second paragraph of Canon 1507 is of no great practical importance in the present study. As regards judicial fees the ruling of Canon 1909 is to be observed. At first blush the regulations of these two canons seem to be identical. There is, however, an appreciable difference. Canon 1507, § 1, clearly states that the list of fees determined upon by the bishops is to be transmitted to the Holy See for approbation. Until this approval is granted the schedule remains ineffective. In Canon 1909 no such requirement is stated. Hence we can conclude that papal approbation is not necessary for the list of judicial fees.[1]

---

[1] Vermeersch-Creusen II, n. 827.

CHAPTER VIII.

Prescription.

1. In Roman Law.

It is a natural and immutable principle that the owner of a thing shall remain so and enjoy all the rights thereof until his property is divested either by his voluntary act of alienation or by some recognized process of law. A person who has been in possession of a thing for a long time is generally regarded as its owner, and this for two reasons: men are naturally careful not to give up whatever belongs to them; and secondly the stability of society necessitates that a possessor be not regarded as a usurper. However, if these presumptions are invariably carried to their ultimate conclusions injustices are bound to arise at times. Hence arbitrary rules with legal sanction have been devised whereby a time is prescribed within which those who claim to be owners, but are not in possession, shall prove their rights; or after the lapse of which, possessors who have observed the requirements of law and who have not been deprived of the property or rights in question shall be recognized as enjoying legitimate ownership. Prescription under some such form or name has existed in the laws of most civilized nations with the possible exception of the Jewish.[1]

During the first centuries of Roman law legislation on usucapion developed and changed in important aspects. In virtue of the law of the XII Tables defects in title were cured by a certain lapse of time.[2] If a person possessed an object in good faith for two years in the case of lands and for one year in

---

[1] Angell, N., *A Treatise on the Limitation of Actions,* (Boston, 1876) 5. Broom, W., *Selections of Legal Maxims,* (London, 1911) 690. Domat-Strahan, J., *The Civil Law in its Natural Order,* (Boston, 1850) 2183. Devas, C., *Political Economy,* (London, 1901) 491.

[2] Cicero, *Topica,* 4, 23, "Usus auctoritas fundi bienniem est........ ceterarum rerum........annus usus est." Ferrini, C., *Manuale di Pandette,* n. 314.

the case of movables he was recognized as owner in law.[1] The brevity of the time required is explained by the fact that the state was small and the control of property closer than in later times. This mode of acquisition, giving quiritary ownership and available to citizens only, was known as usucapion. It applied to both "res mancipi et non mancipi."[2] Being limited to Italian soil it could not be invoked in the case of provincial lands.[3]

With the progress of the centuries and the extension of Roman dominions a more feasible mode of acquiring ownership by lapse of time was developed. This was known as the "longi temporis praescriptio,"[4] and was available to protect the possessory title of anyone, even non-citizens. It gave pretorian possession, but not full ownership. At first it operated only by way of limitation of action as a defense in a suit against claimants. Subsequently it was considered as a mode of acquisition in all cases.[5] In addition, the time period was considerably longer than in the preceding form of legislation; three years for prescription of movables; for immovables, ten years if the parties were present, twenty if they were absent. Thus the old legislation was supplemented and extended to meet the exigencies of the ever-enlarging domains of Rome. By gradual changes the impracticable elements were discarded and new laws added as times and circumstances required. The *Lex Atinia,* passed about the middle of the second century B. C., forbade the extension of prescription to cases of adverse possession;[6] the *Leges Iulia et Plautia* prohibited forcible possession from conferring a right of prescription;[7] while the *Lex Scribonia* included services under the law.[8] When Justinian became Emperor the law of prescription was in need of revision because of a few seemingly obsolete and conflicting remnants of older legislation. It was clear that the short period of time required offered many opportunities for fraudulent practices; movables could still be acquired under the old

[1] Gaius 2, 42; 54; 204. Ulpian, *Regula* 19, 8. Ferrini n. 313; Buckland 242; Sherman, II, 646.

[2] Gaius 2, 46.

[3] Gaius 2, 46. Ulpian, *Regula,* 19, 8. Colquhoun 1117.

[4] C. 7, 33, 1.

[5] Buckland, 249.

[6] Julianus, *Digest* 41, 3, 33 pr. Paulus, *Digest,* 31, 3, 4, 6. Paulus, *Digest,* 50, 16, 215. Cicero, *In Verrem,* I, 42. Ferrini, n. 315. Bruns, *Fontes Iuris Romani Antiqui,* 47.

[7] Gaius, 2, 45. Ferrini, n. 315.

[8] Paulus, *Dig.* 41, 3, 4, 29.

civil law of usucapion in one year, while most of the soil of the Eastern Empire remained provincial so that the two-year period of usucapion was without application. Justinian accordingly abolished the old legal distinction between Italian and provincial soil, altered the period of time required and upon the analogy of the limitations of actions of Theodosius II, enacted that thirty years' possession of property should confer ownership.[1] Thenceforward movables could be prescribed after three years; immovables after ten or twenty years in ordinary, and after thirty years in extraordinary prescription.[2] As an exception the property of the Roman Church could be prescribed only after one hundred years.[3]

The requisites for prescription were five in number, namely:—good faith, not, however, the continuous good faith required by Canon Law but good faith only at the beginning of possession;[4] a just title, that is the prescriptive claimant must have acquired possession in a lawful manner and must hold the property as his own;[5] continuous possession, neither naturally nor legally interrupted;[6] legal period of time, which was three, ten or twenty years in ordinary prescription;[7] and forty years in extraordinary prescription;[8] and finally a prescriptible object.[9] Thus things exempted from commerce, "res extra commercium," were incapable of being prescribed.[10] Other objects such as dotal property, during marriage,[11] property of wards and minors during their guardianship;[12] fiscal property,[13] and in late law, land devoted to religion or charitable purposes were likewise not subject to prescription.[14]

---

[1] *Code* 7, 39, 8, 1.

[2] *Code* 7, 39, 8, 1.

[3] *Code*, 1, 2, 23, 2. *Novellae* 9.

[4] Gaius 2, 43. *Code* 7, 31, 3. *Inst.* 2, 6 pr. *Dig.* 41, 4, 6, 4; 41, 3, 15, 2; 50, 16, 109; 50, 17, 137.

[5] *Code* 7, 31, 3. *Dig.* 41, 3, 27. *Code* 3, 32, 24; 7, 14, 6; 7, 29, 4. Ferrini n. 316.

[6] *Dig.* 41, 2, 23 pr.; 41, 3, 15, 2; 41, 3, 40. *Code* 7, 32, 10; 7, 40, 2.

[7] *Inst.* 2, 6 pr. *Code* 7, 31; 7, 33, 12. *Novellae* 119, 6.

[8] *Code* 7, 39, 8, 1.

[9] *Inst.* 2, 6, 1. *Dig.* 41, 3, 9.

[10] *Inst.* 2, 6, 1. *Dig.* 41, 3, 9.

[11] *Code* 5, 12, 30. *Dig.* 23, 5, 16.

[12] *Code* 7, 35, 3; 2, 40, 2. *Dig.* 41, 1, 48; 27, 5, 2.

[13] *Code* 7, 38, 2. *Dig.* 41, 3, 18.

[14] *Nov.* 111, 1; 131, 6.

2. Prescription in Canon Law.

Canon 1508.

Praescriptionem, tanquam acquirendi et se liberandi modum, prout est in legislatione civili respectivae nationis, Ecclesia pro bonis ecclesiasticis recipit, salvo praescripto canonum qui sequuntur.

The Romans found it necessary to formulate laws of prescription for the maintenance of social tranquillity and the public good which postulated that the rights of property should be fixed,[1] that lawsuits and controversies be definitely settled,[2] that rightful possessors be rewarded with legal assurance of security,[3] and that culpably negligent owners be punished for their carelessness.[4] For practically the same reasons Canon Law has sanctioned the policy of prescription. This is attested by Pope Alexander III (1159–1181):—"Legislator solum propter vitandum miserorum segnitiem et longi temporis errorem et confusionem primus tricennali et quadrangenali praescriptioni vigorem imposuit."[5]

The earliest extant church legislation on prescription is found in the Council of Chalcedon where the period of thirty years is alluded to as sufficient to constitute grounds for prescriptive action.[6] The Council of Arles likewise contained a reference to prescription, although this is somewhat indefinite;[7] the II Council of Seville decided that prescription was not to be computed during times of hostilities;[8] while the IV Council of Toledo recognized prescription of thirty years.[9]

The various references to prescription in the Decree of Gratian indicate the importance of the subject at a comparatively early date.[10] In all this legislation the efforts of popes and councils to adhere to the principles of Roman law are evident, but the attempts are not always successful due to the incorrect

---

[1] *Dig.* 41, 3, 1. *Inst.* 2, 6 pr. Gaius, 2 44.
[2] *Dig.* 41, 10, 5.
[3] *Code* 7, 39, 7 pr.
[4] *Code* 7, 40, 2 pr.
[5] C. 5, X, *De praescriptionibus*, II, 26. Reiffenstuel II, 26, 1, 19.
[6] C. Chalcedonensis (451), Can. 17, *Ss. Conc.* VI, 1228.
[7] C. Aurelianense (511), can. 23, *Ss. Conc.* VIII, 355.
[8] C. Hispalense II, (619) can. 1. *Ss. Conc.* X, 557.
[9] C. Toletanum IV (633), can. 33–34, *Ss. Conc.* X, 628.
[10] C. 1–17, C. XVI, q. 3. C. 1–3, C. XVI, q. 4.

interpretation of the sources and confused ideas as to the meaning and extent of the various laws.[4] Ordinary and extraordinary prescription were often confused by arbitrary quotations and unreliable interpretations of difficult texts.[1] Other reasons for confusion were that Canon law necessarily departed from Roman law in some instances. Thus Canon law insisted on good faith during the entire period of prescriptive possession and required a more secure title than was necessary in Roman law.[2] The similarities and differences of prescription in Roman and Canon law were such that unlearned and careless glossators could easily confuse the two, thus rendering it difficult for succeeding legislators to formulate uniform new laws with conflicting regulations as precedents. Moreover, from the seventh to the twelfth century Germanic and Lombardic laws influenced Canon law to a considerable extent.[3] These laws differed from Roman law on principles of prescription and still they were incorporated in part in legislation of the Church. Even allusions to Scripture were resorted to in an effort to settle questions and reconcile conflicting opinions, with the inevitable result of confusion.

With revived interest in Roman law in the eleventh and twelfth centuries at the great seats of learning of Bologna, Padua, Pavia and Verona a clearer conception of the principles of prescription was made possible. It was then that Canon law formulated its rulings on prescription, based on Roman law, with the modifications possible only in a legal system where conscience is paramount. Subsequent legislation, especially that of Alexander III, Innocent III and Boniface VIII clarified and systematized to a remarkable extent the Church's laws on both acquisitive and liberative prescription.[5] The Council of Trent made no appreciable change in the legislation on prescription.[6] After the Council, especially during the eighteenth and nineteenth centuries, minor details were developed and clarified in

---

[1] C. 4, 16, C. XVI, q. 3. C. 1, 3, C. XVI, q. 4.

[2] C. 15, C. XVI, q. 3.

[3] Vinogradoff, *Roman Law in Medieval Europe*, 42.

[4] C. 13–15, C. XVI, q. 3.

[5] C. 4–20, X, *de praescriptionibus*, II, 26. C. 1–2, *de praescriptionibus*, II, in VI°.

[6] Restrictive legislation was enacted about prescription of the "Iuspatronatus," but this referred only indirectly to prescription. Sess. XXV, *de ref.*, c. 9.

the decisions of the Roman Curia,[1] and in the works of noted commentators.[2]

In conformity with its previous legislation the Church continues to recognize prescription as a just means of acquiring rights or liberating one from obligations provided the rulings of Canon law are respected. Before the Code, as intimated above, the general basis for the rules of ecclesiastical prescription was Roman law, modified to conform to the spirit of the Church.[3] Since the Code, however, Canon law no longer depends upon Roman law to correct its deficiencies or supplement its lacunae.[4] Canon law has reached such a stage of development that it is no longer dependent upon other legal systems. It can, however, and this is not at all derogatory to the merits of any legal system, canonize certain portions of civil laws when it sees fit; thereby accepting them as its own and incorporating them as a part of its law.[5] The greater part of the Church's legislation on prescription is an instance of this adoption or canonization of civil law. Thus Canon 1508 declares that the Church recognizes the enactments of civil law in matters of prescription provided these do not violate rulings of Canons 1508–1512.

3. Requirements for Prescription.

Canon law requires that five conditions be fulfilled before prescription be invoked. The existence of these must be proved, not presumed.[6] First of all the object must be prescriptible.

---

[1] S. C. C., *Imolen.*, *Solutionis Legati*, 22 Martii 1873; *Thesaurus*, CXXXII (1873), 287. S. C. C., *Pisauren.*, *Decimarum et Erectionis Fontis Baptismalis*, 5 Martii 1892; *Thesaurus*, CLI (1892) 198. S. C. C., *S. Claudii*, *Juris ad S. Reliquiam*, 25 Jan. 1902; *Thesaurus*, CLXI, (1902) 78. S. C. C., Romana, *Spolii*, 25 Feb., 1905; *Thesaurus*, CLXIV (1905), 237 S. Rom. Rot., *Romana*, *Salviani*, 9 Feb. 1688; *Decis S. Rom. Rot. Nup.* Dec. 94, n. 11, II, 127. S. Rom. Rot., *Neapolitana*, *Pecuniaria*, 10 Maii 1694; *Decis. S. Rom. Rot. Nup.* Dec. 235, n. 2, IV. 332.

[2] Fagnanus II, 26. Schmalzgrueber II, 26. Reiffenstuel II, 26. Barbosa, *De officio et potestate episcopi*, Alleg. 129. De Lugo, *De justitia et jure*, Disp. VII.

[3] C. 1, X, *de novi operis nunciatione*, V, 32. Benedictus XIV, *De Synodo Dioecesana*, Lib. IX. Fagnanus II, 26, 10, n. 18. Suarez, *De legibus*, III, c. 8, n. 3. Bouix, *De judiciis ecclesiasticis*, I, 19. Soglia I, n. 44. D'Annibale I, n. 201. Wernz I, 195.

[4] This does not exclude the possibility of considering Roman law as an important subsidiary science aiding the study of the history and development of Canon law. Maroto I, n. 383.

[5] Maroto I, n. 381–384.

[6] Lega, *De judiciis ecclesiasticis*, n. 288. Wernz III, n. 301. Lehmkuhl I, n. 922.

Some things cannot be subject to prescription because of their very nature, the prohibitions of Canon law or the personal incapability of the person seeking prescription.[1] Secondly, good faith is requisite not only in the beginning but throughout the entire term of prescription as declared by the IV Council of the Lateran[2] and now required by Canon 1512. Thirdly, a just title is necessary as was required in the law of the Decretals.[3] This is not expressly demanded by the Code, but it is implicitly necessary, for possession must begin with a title of some sort.[4] Fourthly, just possession is necessary in accordance with the legal maxim: "sine possessione praescriptio non procedit."[5] This necessitates public, peaceable and safe possession and hence precludes the possibility of invoking prescription in cases of forcible, secret and precarious possession. Moreover, the person invoking prescription must hold the property in his own name; and his possession should be continuous, that is, neither interrupted nor suspended.[6] Finally the time required by law must be fulfilled.

For some objects the time period is specified in Canon 1511; for others the enactments of the Civil laws of each country must be followed whenever the objects in question come within the scope of civil jurisdiction.[7] Here a twofold difficulty presents itself. On the one hand many civil codes of late years are silent on the subject of the time limit for prescription; while the requisite periods as stated by the others are so extremely variant that they defy any kind of summary. In this country there is little uniformity among the States in the matter. For the prescription of immovables five years is sufficient in California; in Tennessee, South Carolina, North Carolina, Georgia and Florida seven years

---

[1] S. C. C., *Neapolitana, Visitationis*, 9 Sept., 1882; *Thesaurus*, CXLI (1882), 603. S. C. C., *Papiensis, Exemptionis*, 8 Martii 1884; *Thesaurus*, CXLIII (1884), 265. S. C. C., *Civitatis Plebis, Onerum*, 2 Aprilis 1887; *Thesaurus*, CXLVI (1887) 161.

[2] C. 20, X, *de praescriptionibus*, II, 26. C. 1, *de praescriptionibus*, II, 13 in VI.° Giraldus, II, Sectio 280, p. 189.

[3] C. 17, X, *de praescriptionibus*, II, 26. La Croix III, 2. n. 498.

[4] Cocchi VI, 367.

Canon 1446 legalizes an exceptional form of prescription in virtue of which peaceful possession of a benefice in good faith for three years with a title, even though invalid, suffices for the securing of the benefice by lawful prescription. However, prescription could not operate without any title whatsoever or with a title vitiated by simony.

[5] Reg. 3, R. J. in VI°. Wernz III, 301.

[6] Wernz III, 302.

[7] Bouvier, v. *Limitations*, II, 1998–2021.

are required; in Indiana, Michigan, Mississippi and Nevada fifteen years; in Kansas, Nebraska, Ohio, and Pennsylvania twenty-one years; in Maine forty years, while in the other States twenty years is the regular time requirement.[1]

4. Objects Exempted from Prescription.

The power of withholding or withdrawing objects from the ordinary course of prescriptive action by positive enactment is recognized as belonging to every supreme legislator. In Roman law "res juris divini," "res fiscales" and "res dotales" under certain conditions were among the objects withheld from the operation of prescription.[2] The Church is cognizant of its right to withhold or declare objects exempt from prescription. Accordingly Canon 1509 enumerates four objects referring to liberative,[3] and four to acquisitive prescription that are not subject to the operation of prescriptive means.[4]

Canon 1509.

Praescriptioni obnoxia non sunt: 1°. Quae sunt iuris divini sive naturalis sive positivi.

Those things that are of divine law, whether natural or positive, are not subject to prescription for they are beyond the control of human agencies. Thus an article secured by theft could never be gained by prescription nor could a laic obtain the power and jurisdiction of hearing confessions by prescriptive processes.[5]

2°. Quae obtineri possunt ex solo privilegio apostolico.

Rights that are granted only by Apostolic indult are likewise exempted from prescription. Thus simple priests of the Latin Rite cannot secure the right of conferring Confirmation, no matter how long they have attempted to perform the rite.

---

[1] Bouvier, v. *Prescription,* III, 2671–2673.

It is to be borne in mind that English Law and several particular statutes of States in this country distinguish between prescription proper which transfers property or extinguishes obligations; and mere limitation of action which, leaving rights and obligations intact, simply withdraws legal support.

[2] Gaius 2, 48. *Digest* 41, 3, 9. *Code* 7, 35, 3.

[3] n. 1, 5, 7, 8.

[4] n. 2, 3, 4, 6.

[5] Ferraris, v. *Usucapio,* I, n. 43. De Lugo, *De justitia et jure,* Disp. VII, Sect. 8, n. 143. Wernz III, n. 299.

Innocent III sternly reprehended the priests of Constantinople for trying to arrogate such a right to themselves.[1]

3°. Iura spiritualia, quorum laici non sunt capaces, si agatur de praescriptione in commodum laicorum.

There are many rights in the Church which, by their very nature, are incapable of attainment by laics, such as spiritual rights or those inseparably joined to spiritualities. Thus, for instance, a laic cannot obtain prescriptive rights to tithes.[2] The qualifying phrase "si agatur de praescriptione in commodum laicorum" removes all doubt as to the possible extent of the law.[3]

4°. Fines certi et indubii provinciarum ecclesiasticarum, dioecesium, paroeciarum, vicariatuum apostolicorum, praefecturarum apostolicarum, abbatiarum vel praelaturarum *nullius*.

To avoid confusion and endless controversy, the Church has found it necessary to declare as non-prescriptible the limits of provinces, dioceses, parishes, apostolic vicariates, apostolic prefectures, abbacies and prelacies "nullius," when these have once been defined certainly and definitely.[4] It is to be observed that the boundaries must be certain in order to preclude prescription. In certain instances where boundaries are not defined, prescription can well be a means of settling doubts and determining boundaries as was the case of our own country in the pioneer days, when diocesan limits could not be strictly determined by the Congregation of Propaganda before the territories were correctly surveyed.

5°. Eleemosynae et onera Missarum.

In virtue of the Canon 1509, 5°, excluding Mass stipends and obligations from prescription a mutual security is established between the giver of the stipend and the one obliged to say the Masses.[5] It is still possible, as maintained by Wernz before the

[1] C 4, X, *de consuetudine*, I, n. 4.

[2] Canon 118. C. 7, X, *de praescriptionibus*, II, 26. Schmalzgrueber II, *26, 3, n. 51.* Santi II, *26, n. 6.*

[3] Ferraris, v. *Usucapio*, I, n. 16.

[4] C. Hispalense II, (619), can. 2, *Ss. Conc.* X, 557. C. 5, 6, C. XVI, q. 3. C. 4, X, *de parochis et alienis parochianis*, III, 29. S. C. C., *Neapolitana et Puterlana, Jurisdictio*, 22 Aprilis 1882; *Thesaurus*, CXLI, (1882), 190. Reiffenstuel II, 26, n. 40.

[5] Conc. Trident., sess. XXV, *de ref.*, c. 5. S. C. C., *Civitatis Plebis, Onerum*, 2 Aprilis 1887; *Thesaurus*, CXLVI (1887), 161. D'Annibale II, 151; III, n. 76, nota 14. Wernz III, n. 300. *Analect. Eccl.* IX, 201.

The possibility of the prescription of the number and obligation of Masses

Code,[1] for the obligation of celebrating Masses to be transferred by prescriptive action from one priest or community to another.[2] Before the Code only the obligations of Masses were considered as not subject to prescription.[3] Now both offerings and obligations are declared as exempted.

6°. Beneficium ecclesiasticum sine titulo.

According to Canon 147, § 1, an ecclesiastical office cannot be obtained without canonical provision,[4] which requires that the office be granted by competent ecclesiastical authority in conformity with Canon law. Canon 1509, 6°, declares that prescription cannot be invoked in the case of an ecclesiastical benefice obtained without a title, at least a colored title. This positive provision of law is evidently intended to forestall attempts to secure benefices in bad faith through legal artifice and technical fraud.[5]

7°. Ius visitationis et obedientiae, ita ut subditi a nullo Praelato visitari possint et nulli Praelato iam subsint.

From centuries of experience the Church has learned that obedience to legitimate superiors and visitations by them are means necessary to insure order and respect for authority. Consequently, it considers these not subject to prescription, for there is a headship in the Church to which all members, individually or in groups, must be subservient, as declared by Innocent III,[6]

[1] III, n. 300.

[2] Vermeersch-Creusen II, n. 830.

[3] Wernz III, n. 300.

[4] Reg. 1, R. J., in VI°.

[5] In accordance with Canon 1446 peaceful possession of a benefice in good faith for three years with a title, even though invalid, suffices for its acquisition by lawful prescription. Without a title or with a title vitiated by simony the longest possession would remain ineffective. C. un., *de sequestratione possessionum et fructuum*, II, 6, in Clem.

[6] C. 12, X, *de praescriptionibus*, II, 26. C. 16, X, *de praescriptionibus*, II, 26.

was once mooted among authors. Some commentators as Gobat, Tusch, Tamburini, La Croix, (IV, n. 852) and Dicastillo (De justitia et jure, Lib. II, t. I, d. 1, n. 262) were of the opinion that the number and obligations of Masses were prescriptible.

Others as Felix Potestas (Tom. I, Pars. II, n. 2335) and Manocelli (*Formularium legale practicum fori ecclesiae*, Romae 17° 6, Pars. IV, Suppl. ad Tom. II, n. 55) maintained that the number and obligations of Masses did not admit of prescription. They likened souls in purgatory to wards in Roman law, and hence as orphans in need of Masses could not have their rights prescribed. This latter opinion was accepted by D'Annibale and Wernz and is now adopted by the Code.

and recognized throughout the world since that time.[1] Canon 1509, 7°, excludes extinctive prescription of visitation and obedience, but in no way prohibits translative prescription in virtue of which rights of visitation and obedience could be transferred from one prelate to another.[2] Formerly a vexed question in this connection was the prescription of the procurations given at the time of the visit.[3] This, however, is no longer of vital importance because of the change of legislation on the matter.[4]

8°. Solutio cathedratici.

As stated in Canon 1504, the cathedraticum is exacted "in signum subjectionis." Since the prelate's right to obedience cannot be prescribed, it follows that the tax given as a sign of subjection must likewise be excluded from prescription.[5]

5. The Prescription of Sacred Objects.

Canon 1510.

§1. Res sacrae quae in dominio privatorum sunt, praescriptione acquiri a privatis personis possunt, quae tamen eas adhibere nequeunt ad profanos usus; si vero consecrationem vel benedictionem amiserint, libere acquiri possunt etiam ad usus profanos, non tamen sordidos.

§2. Res sacrae, quae in dominio privatorum non sunt, non a persona privata, sed a persona morali ecclesiastica contra aliam personam moralem ecclesiasticam praescribi possunt.

Sacred things[6] belonging to an individual can be prescribed by another individual, but they may not be employed for profane uses: "Semel Deo dicatum non est ad usus humanos ulterius transferendum."[7] This ruling about the proper use of sacred things is in accord with Canon 1150 which enjoins that consecrated or blessed objects should be reverently handled and not

[1] C. Ravennatense III (1314), cap. VIII, *Ss. Conc.* XXV, 542. S. C. C., *Neapolitana, Visitationis*, 9 Sept. 1882; *Thesaurus*, CXLI, (1882) 603. S. C. C., *Papiensis, Exemptionis*, 8 Martii 1884; *Thesaurus*, CXLIII, (1884) 265. Barbosa, *De officio et potestate episcopi*, Alleg. 129, n. 9. Reiffenstuel II, 26, n. 49. Schmalzgrueber II, 26, III, n. 51. Ferraris, v. *Usucapio*, I, n. 40.

[2] Barbosa, *De officio et potestate episcopi*, Alleg. 128, n. 3–5; 129, 8-9. Reiffenstuel II, 26, n. 53. Santi II, 26, n. 7.

[3] Schmalzgrueber III, 39, IV, n. 112–116. Giraldus II, Tom. I, Pars. I, Sectio 284. Pirhing II, 26, V. D'Annibale II, n. 151, nota 4. Richter, *Canones et Decreta Concilii Tridentini*, 335.

[4] C. 16, X, *de praescriptionibus*, II, 26. Canon 346.

[5] Canon 1509, 8°. Conc. Romanum (1725), Tit VIII, cap. 4. Benedictus XIV, *De synodo dioecesana*, V, cap. VII, n. 6. Reiffenstuel III, 39, II, n. 16.

[6] Canon 1497, §2.

[7] Reg. 51, R. J., in VI.°

put to profane uses even if they are in the possession of individuals. If, however, the sacred objects have lost their blessing or consecration,[1] they may be freely acquired for profane, but not for unbecoming uses and may be consecrated or blessed anew provided the proper formalities are observed.

In the decretal legislation there was no explicit mention nor definite regulation governing the prescription of sacred objects; nor was it clearly determined what things were included under the term "res sacrae." Consequently, commentators trying to reconcile excerpts of Canon and Roman law confused the matter considerably with variant opinions. Fagnanus[2] and Schmalzgreuber maintained that "res sacrae" such as chalices, vestments and altars; "res religiosae," tombs and the like; "res sanctae," such as walls and gates of cities, were not subject to prescription by anyone.[3] This same opinion was held by Sebastianelli.[4] Reiffenstuel, without defining the terms, considered "res sacrae" as capable of prescription by laics as well as clerics;[5] Ferraris denied that laics could prescribe "res sacrae"[6] while Pirhing,[7] La Croix,[8] and Santi[9] held "res sacrae" to be incapable of prescription by anyone. During the latter part of the nineteenth century, the opinions of theologians and canonists became clearer and more uniform, both as regards terminology and the application of the laws of prescription to sacred things.[10]

It is to be especially noted that the first paragraph of Canon 1510 refers only to individuals—"privati"—. Vermeersch is of the opinion that the term "privatus" is equivalent to "laicus" in this instance. This view is not held by other commentators and seems hardly in conformity with the context and the general intent of the Canon.[11]

---

[1] Canon 1305, §1.

[2] II, 26, n. 12.

[3] II, 26, II, n. 25.

[4] *De Rebus*, p. 370, n. 390.

[5] II, 26, I, n. 34.

[6] V. *Usucapio*, I, n. 15.

[7] II, 26, III.

[8] III, Pars II, n. 501.

[9] II, 26, n. 6.

[10] The opinions of Lehmkuhl, (I, n. 918); Lega (*De Jud. Eccl.* I, 269); and particularly Wernz (III, 299, nota 16) were in close conformity with the present legislation of the Code.

[11] Blat, Lib. III Pars. VI, p. 510: "privatorum, nempe personarum physicarum, etsi ad clericorum sacerdotumve patrimonium vel quasi-patrimonium pertineant."

The terminology of this Canon is adapted to a great extent from Wernz, III,

Sacred things which are not in the possession of private persons cannot be prescribed by a private person. They can, however, be prescribed by one ecclesiastical corporation against another, whether these moral persons be collegiate or noncollegiate.[1] Nor is there any legal restriction preventing a juridical ecclesiastical person from prescribing sacred things against an individual.[2]

6. Time Period and Good Faith Necessary for Prescription.

Canon 1511.

§ 1. Res immobiles, mobiles pretiosae, iura et actiones sive personales sive reales, quae pertinent ad Sedem Apostolicam, spatio centum annorum praescribuntur.

§ 2. Quae ad aliam personam moralem ecclesiasticam, spatio triginta annorum.

Canon 1512.

Nulla valet praescriptio, nisi bona fide nitatur, non solum initio possessionis, sed toto possessionis tempore ad praescriptionem requisito.

Immovable objects, movable articles that are precious, rights and actions whether personal or real which pertain to the Apostolic See[3] are prescriptible only after a period of one hundred years. It is to be noted that only movable articles that are precious come under the ruling of this privileged time. This period, the same as accorded the Roman Church by the Emperor Justinian,[4] is uniformly insisted on by all the Pontiffs legislating on the matter.[5]

Whenever the objects, rights and actions mentioned above

---

[1] Canon 99.

C. 6, X, *de praescriptionibus*, II, 26. Wernz III, n. 299, nota 16.

[2] C. 3, X, *de praescriptionibus*, II, 26. Schmalzgrueber II, 26, n. 103.

[3] Canon 7; 100, §1; 262.

[4] *Novellae* 9.

[5] C. 16, 17, C. XVI, q. 3. C. 13, 14, 17, X, *de praescriptionibus*, II, 26. C. 4, X, *de confirmatione utili vel inutili*, II, 30. C. 2, *de praescriptionibus*, II, 13, in VI°. Honorius III, ep. *Sedis apostolicae*, 23 Aprilis 1221; Fontes, n. 32. Benedictus XIV, const. *Ad honorandum*, 27 Martii 1752; Fontes, n. 420.

The declarations of Honorius III and Benedict XIV emphasize the fact that the Church of the Lateran, considered as a special part of Papal property, enjoys the right of a prescriptive period of one hundred years.

---

n. 299, nota 16, where the word "privatus" is hardly equivalent to "laicus." The term "in dominio privati" as employed by Wernz is intended to retain, as far as possible, the meaning it had in Roman law where it certainly was not used as a synonym for laic in contradistinction to clerics.

belong to other church corporations they can be prescribed after thirty years. This period was not definitively invariable before the Code. Thirty years was the time often mentioned in decretal and post-decretal laws;[1] but since the eighteenth century the period of forty years[2] was almost uniformly insisted on in decisions[3] and generally accepted by commentators.[4] The reasons for the change of the law of the Code to thirty years are not mentioned by recent commentators. It is significant to note that the term of forty years was retained in the *Schema Codicis* of 1913. A desire to bring this Canon into closer conformity with the European civil laws—which generally require thirty years as suggested by the Bishop of Breslau—[5] may have motivated the change.

The privileges granted to some religious Orders whereby their property is secured by a longer prescriptive period, viz., sixty years for the Benedictines and Camalduli Monks, and one hundred years for the Cistercians and Mendicants, have not been abrogated by the Code.[6]

Canon 1512 indicates one point where Canon law is decidedly different from Roman law and the civil law of most nations. These legal systems demand that good faith exist only at the beginning of prescription. For reasons of legal expediency this is as much as can be required, or at least ascertained in many

---

[1] C. 1, 4, 8, 9, 15, C. XVI, q. 3. C. 13, X, *de praescriptionibus*, II, 26. S. R. Rotae, *Neapolitana, Pecuniaria*, 10 Maii 1694; *Decis S. R. Rotae Nuper.*, Decis, 235, n. 2.

[2] C. 2, *de praescriptionibus*, II, 13, in VI°.

[3] S. C. C., *Nullius-Altamurae, Divisionis*, 13 Aug. 1870; *Thesaurus*, CXXIX (1870) 419. S. C. C., *Mantuana, Jurispatronatus*, 22 Junii 1872; *Thesaurus*, CXXXI, (1872) 341. S. C. C., *Imolen, Solutionis legati*, 22 Martii 1873; *Thesaurus*, CXXXII (1873) 277. S. C. C., *Spoletana, Annuae praestationis*, 24 Apriolis 1875; *Thesaurus*, CXXXIV (1875) 246. S. C. C., *Gaudisien, Onerum*, 29 Febr. 1896; *Thesaurus*, CLV (1896) 147. S. C.C., *St. Claudis, Juris ad S. Reliquiam* 25 Jan. 1902; *Thesaurus*, CLXI (1902) 78. S. C. C. *Nullius seu Montis Cassini, Jurium*, 22 Martii 1902; *Thesaurus*, CLXI (1902) 268. S. C. C., *Romana, Spolii*, 25 Febr. 1905; *Thesaurus*, CXIV (1905) 237.

[4] Fagnanus III, 29, n. 1–3. Schmalzgrueber II, 26; III, n. 102. Ferraris, v. *Usucapio*, n. 15. Reiffenstuel, II, 26, n. 163. Giraldus II, 26, Sectio 280. Pirhing II, 26, Sectio III. De Lugo, *De justitia et jure*, Disp. VII, Sect. VI, n. 73. La Croix II, 227. Sebastianelli, *De rebus*, 378. D'Annibale II, n. 139, 150. Wernz III, n. 304.

[5] *Animadversiones III Lib. Codicis Schematis*, in Canon 788.
Canon 788 of the *Schema* corresponds to Canon 1511

[6] S. Rom. Rotae, *Romana. Salviani*, 9 Febr. 1688; *Decis, S. Rom. Rot. Nuper.*, Dec. 94, n. 11. Schmalzgrueber II, 26, III, n. 101. Reiffenstuel II, 26, n. 163. Vermeersch-Creusen II, n. 831.

cases in practice. The Church's law exalts conscience and emphasizes the personal responsibility of each individual not only before the court of law, but before God. Hence, Canon law can insist more determinately on the perdurance of good faith during the entire period of prescription. This notable change from Roman law was insisted on from the earliest times by the Church.[1]

The legislation of the Code on the matter of prescription is nothing short of remarkable in comparison with the older laws. The rulings governing prescription have been clarified and simplified, so that the legal principles are not only more precise, but the danger of endless conflicts with civil statutes has been happily obviated to a notable extent. Before the Code a maze of conflicting and all but irreconcilable principles confronted one on every side. Extraneous fragments of Roman law were clung to by some commentators; civil laws—oftentimes irrevelant—were cited by others, with the inevitable result of confusion. The legislation of the Code is not without its own difficulties, but it has at least laid down the principles along which a clear and easily applied body of laws can be perfected for the furtherance of harmony and justice.

---

[1] C. 5, 17, 20, X, *de praescriptionibus*, II, 26. Reg. 2, R. J., in VI°. S. Rom. Rotae, *Romana, Sucessionis*, 28 Jan. 1686; *Decis. S. R. Rotae Nuper.*, Decis 256 n. 11. S. Rom. Rotae, *Melevitana, Antianitatis*, 14 Jun. 1694; *Decis. S. R. Rotae Nuper.*, Decis 254, n. 10. S. Rom. Rotae, *Vercellen, Annexae praestationis*, 22 Jun. 1701; *Decis. S. R. Rotae Nuper.*, Decis 161, n. 10. S. C. C. *Imolen, Solutionis legati*, 22 Martii 1873; *Thesaurus*, CXXXII (1873) 287. S. C. C. *Nullius, Reductionis canonis*, 28 Martii 1874; *Thesaurus*, CXXXIII (1874) 177. S. C. C. *Nullius, Facultatis*, 12 Sept. 1874; *Thesaurus*, CXXXIII (1874) 538.

CHAPTER IX.

Donations and Bequests in Favor of Religion and Charity.

1. Evolution of Testamentary Legislation.

From the earliest times civilized societies recognized the right which empowers a man to regulate the disposition of his property after death.[1] The fundamental idea which lies at the root of proprietary rights is that of immortality. An owner may die but his ownership survives and should be capable of transfer in some way, for property is not destroyed by the death of the proprietor.[2] The object of laws concerning wills was to enable owners of property to control its disposition at their decease. The chief purpose of legislation then was to cause the intentions and wishes of owners to be expressed and their expression to be so preserved and manifested that they could be ascertained.[3]

The precise source whence a will derives its effect has long been mooted among lawyers and theologians.[4] "Some hold that the power of testamentary disposition is derived from the law of nature, inasmuch as there is nothing to prevent a man from doing some act and at the same time suspending its effect until after his death. Others maintain that the will of a person cannot produce its effect until the testator be dead. They conclude then that the power of testamentary disposition is derived from positive law. We may, perhaps, hold as certain that the law of nature gives owners of property the right to dispose of it in some way in view of death but that it does not determine of itself the method of disposition by will. This precise method is a result of the determination of the natural by positive law."[5]

---

[1] Shouler, J., *Law of Executors and Administration of Wills*, 12–14. Maine, H., *L'ancien droit*, 187. Greiff, L., *De l'origine du testament romain*, 188. *American and English Encyclopedia of Law*, XXIX, 126.

[2] Leo XIII, ep. encycl. *Quod Apostolici*, 28 Dec. 1878, *Fontes* n. 576.

[3] Carroll v. Carroll, 16 How. 275, 14 U. S. (L. ed.) 936.

[4] Schmalzgrueber III, 26, 1, n. 6.

[5] Slater I, 500. Rood, *Treatise on the Law of Wills*, 7–12.

The Greeks, it appears, were the first to formulate and systematize laws of testation.[1] These were borrowed and perfected by the Romans, whose laws in these matters form the basis of much of the present day legislation.[2] In the first centuries of Roman law the family was the sole owner. Accordingly the death of an individual did not remove the true owner of the property. The members of his family survived and the property rights lived in them. In the course of time the idea of private ownership, in contradistinction to family ownership, began to prevail. The individual owner was then allowed in law to dispose of his property by will, thus asserting his absolute and individual rights of ownership. Consequently testamentary succession supplanted intestate succession to a notable degree.[3]

The primary purpose of a will in Roman law—unlike that of English and American law—was the appointment of an heir.[4] Various other matters could be included, but these did not strictly belong to the essence of the will. In addition two other principles were of fundamental importance in reference to wills. These were: "semel heres, semper heres," and "nemo pro parte testatus;" in virtue of which a person who had once assumed or been invested with the rights of heir could not voluntarily divest himself; while a will had to extend to the whole property of the testator; a part of it could not be devised by will and the rest left to pass on intestacy.[5]

The most ancient forms or wills known in Roman law are mentioned by Gauis as the "testamentum in comitiis calatis" and the "testamentum in procinctu."[6] The first, made by a special legislative act, was an enactment of the popular assembly known as the "comitia curiata," which met twice a year to attest

---

[1] Plato, *De legibus*, II, 679. Demosthenes, *Orat. in Shep.*, II, 983. Bonfante, *Famiglia e Successione*, 337–354.

It is true that sage provisions on testation are found in the Code of Hammurabi, §§ 165–166, 178–179, but these fragmentary statutes cannot be said to constitute a testamentary system.

[2] Redfield, *Wills*, 1–3. Tacitus, *Germaniae*, 20.

[3] For discussion of different views as to priority of succession by will; the devolution of the chieftaincy of the corporate family and similar problems, see Scialoja, *Diritto Ereditario;* Maine, *Ancient Law*, 281; Lenel, *Essays in Legal History*, 230; Buckland, 281.

[4] Gaius 2, 229. *Inst.* 2, 20, 34. *Code* 6, 23, 24. Buckland, 281; Sherman II, 679; Ferrini, n. 610; Cuq, *Les Institutions Juridiques des Romains*, I, 279; Pacchioni, *Corso di Diritto Romanò*, III, 420.

[5] Buckland, 281.

[6] Gaius 2, 101. Ferrini, n. 610; Bonfante, *Istituzione di diritto Romano*, 571; Cuq, 280; Pacchioni, III 421.

and approve such testamentary transfers.[1] The second, permitted because of the impossibility of awaiting the regular assembly, was made at the time of the mobilization of the armies for a campaign.[2] Both of these forms were obsolete before the beginning of the Empire.[3]

The inadequacy of these two forms of wills became apparent at an early period. The need of more convenient forms was filled by the military testament[4] and the mancipatory will, called the "testamentum per aes et libram" from the copper and the scales employed in the ceremony. In virtue of this latter an outright conveyance of entire properties was made in the presence of five witnesses by the ceremony of mancipation.[5] Gradually this form of will changed: discarding many of the features of mancipatory transfers and assuming aspects more closely resembling the secret, written wills of later times. As the process was one of gradual evolution exact dates are not agreed upon by scholars.[6]

Under the pretorian law the irksomeness of the formalities of the mancipatory wills became manifest. Grave injustices frequently resulted from trivial defects of form. This eventually induced the pretors to recognize the necessity of a more practicable form of will.[7] Accordingly a will sealed by seven witnesses was capable of transferring the ownership of property to a designated person. This did not, however, constitute him full heir in the strict acceptation of the word as in early law.[8] This will served as the basis for the final form of written will under Justinian.

In Justinianean law the best features of the testamentary legislation of the Imperial and the ante-Justinianean periods were merged into the tripartite will, so called as deriving its rules from three sources.[9] From civil law it retained the requirements

[1] *Inst.* 2, 10, 1; Ulpian, *Regula*, 20, 2; Muirhead 166.

[2] Cicero, *De natura deorum*, 2, 3. Plutarch, *Vita Coriolani*, 278. Sherman II, 684; Sohm-Ledlie, 542.

[3] *Inst.* 2, 10, 1. Cuq, 1, 521.

[4] Gaius 2, 109. *Inst.* 2, 11, 1.

[5] Gaius 2, 102–104. Ulpian 20, 9. *Cod. Theod.* 4, 4, 3. *Inst.* 2, 10, 1. Pacchioni III, 424.

[6] Lenel, *Essays in Legal History*, 134. Buckland, 283.

For forms of wills see Bruns, *Fontes Iuris Romani antiqui*, 270–282 where copies of ancient wills are reproduced.

[7] *Inst.* 2, 10, 2.

[8] Gaius 2, 119–120. *Inst.* 2, 10, 2.

[9] *Code* 6, 23, 21. Bonfante, *Istituzione*, 573.

of the assemblage of the witnesses and the performance of the formalities at one and the same time;[1] from the Pretorian law the employment of seven witnesses and the affixing of their seals;[2] from the Imperial statutes the requirement of the signature of the testator and the witnesses at the foot of the will.[3] Besides the written will an oral or mancipatory will was valid in Justinianean law. Such a will, if private, required seven witnesses;[4] if public, it was to be declared so before a magistrate.[5]

Canon law has followed Roman law very closely on testamentary legislation. The principles underlying the Roman system on wills were recognized as concise, clear and equitable and not demanding any notable revision by the Church, at least in the first centuries. In addition to this theoretical harmony there were reasons of convenience that prompted ecclesiastical legislators to adhere closely to legislation of Roman law on wills. After the year 321, when the Church's right to be heir was recognized,[6] donations, grants and bequests in its favor became very numerous. Consequently it was not only expedient, but even advantageous for the Church to observe the law under which it was benefiting as a general trustee and beneficiary.[7] After the time of Justinian a certain legal reciprocity was recognized and enforced by the laws of Rome, so that the Church could consider Roman law almost as its own; while Roman law in turn sanctioned the enactments of Church Councils.[8] Under such conditions it was neither feasible nor expedient for the Church to attempt any drastic change in testamentary legislation, at least during the first centuries of Justinianean law.

With the fall of Rome and the consequent infiltration of Germanic, Lombardic and Visigothic factors into the legal prin-

---

[1] "Uno contentu actus," *Dig.* 28, 1, 21, 3. "Uno eodemque tempore," Inst. 2, 10, 3.

[2] Gaius 2, 119. *Inst.* 2, 10, 2.

[3] *Inst.* 2, 10, 3.

[4] *Inst.* 2, 10, 14; *Code* 6, 23, 21, 2; 6, 23, 26.

[5] *Code* 6, 23, 19. Other forms of wills of less importance were: "testamentum pestis tempore," (*Code* 6, 23, 8) allowing the witnesess to attest a will successively during the prevalence of contagious disease without even being in the same room with the sick person; "testamentum ruri conditum" permitting five witnesses in an emergency in the country, (*Code* 6, 28, 8); "testamentum caeci" requiring an eighth witness when a blind person executed a will without a "tabularius," (*Inst.*, 2, 12, 4; *Code* 6, 28, 8.) Sohm-Ledlie, 549. Buckland, 286. Sherman II, 688. Bonfante, *Istituzione*, 574. Pacchioni III, 431.

[6] *Cod. Theod.* 16, 2, 4. *Code* 1, 2, 13; 1, 3, 45.

[7] *Dig.* 1, 3, 45. Colquhoun 916.

[8] *Novellae* 131, 1. *Basilica* 5, 3, 2.

ciples of the Church, ecclesiastical law was of necessity bound to formulate its own distinctive canons on wills and testaments. These in reality differed but little from the fundamental statutes of Roman law.[1] In accordance with the concessions of Justinianean law bishops retained their right to supervise the execution of pious bequests.[2] In this matter great vigilance was necessary for frequently the faithful would disregard the wills benefiting the Church and retain the grants and bequests for themselves. This practice elicited condemnations from popes and councils, and was checked to a great extent by the co-operation of civil with ecclesiastical courts.[3]

For several centuries after the fall of Rome the Church was the only guardian and interpreter of Roman law among the barbaric and unlettered nations of Europe who were engrossed in warfare or busied with the more rudimentary pursuits of life.[4] Hence it is not surprising to find the Church administering justice in behalf of the civil tribunals and at the same time guiding the legislation of the different peoples so as to conform as closely as possible to the safe principles of Roman law. Consequently the Church's legislation on testamentary matters was respected in most courts;[5] while some nations went so far as to empower ecclesiastical tribunals to handle all testamentary cases.[6] In England, for instance, wills affecting property were governed by canon law and administered by the ecclesiastical courts. The power to make such wills existed from time immemorial in England and originated long before the Norman conquest.[7] These

---

[1] Colquhoun 114. Solmi, *Storia Del Diritto Italiano*, 237; 1014.

[2] Solmi, 237.

[3] Gregorius Magnus ad Januarium Epis., *Epist, IX*, Lib. IV, Indict. XII, MPL, LXXVII, 677. C. Carthaginense V (398), can. 95, *Ss. Conc.* III, 958. C. Vasense II (442), can. 4, *Ss. Conc.* VI, 453. C. Aurelianense IV (541), can. 19, *Ss. Conc.* IX, 116. C. Aurelianense V (549), can. 16, *Ss. Conc.* IX, 132. C. Lugdunense II (567), can. 2, *Ss. Conc.* IX, 787. C. Turonense II (567), can. 25, *Ss. Conc.* IX, 804. C. Matisconense I (581), can. 4, *Ss. Conc.* IX, 931. C. Parisiense V (615), can. 10, *Ss. Conc.* X, 541. Thomassinus Par. III, I, cap. 24, n. 3.

[4] Pollock-Maitland I 35, 94–96, 108. Vinogradoff 9–33. Solmi, *Storia del Diritto Italiano*, 503, 724. Schupfer, *Manuale di Storia del Diritto Italiano*, 317.

[5] Pollock-Maitland I, 14, 108. Solmi 237.

[6] *Cambridge Medieval History* II, 143–145.

[7] Hatheway V. Smith, 79 Conn. 65 Atl. 1059, 9 Ann. cas. 99, 9 L. R. A. (N. S.) 310. Buchanan v. Matlock, 8 Humph. (Tenn.) 390, 47 Am. Dec. 622.

concessions were due primarily to the fact that by an almost universal custom the church was remembered in nearly every will.[1] Hence it was a provision of convenience for the states to declare all wills subject to the Church's rules on attestation and execution.[2] As intimated above such laws were adopted in the main from Roman law. There was, however, a notable exception. It was the law considered by Pope Alexander III to be founded on "divine law and the teaching of the Fathers, and sanctioned by a universal custom," which declared two or three witnesses sufficient to attest a will in favor of the Church. This number was determined upon because of the Scriptural teaching that "in the mouth of two or three witnesses every word may stand."[3]

This ruling of Canon law and the Church's authority of supervising the attestation and executing wills were almost universally respected during the Middle Ages. Later these powers were denied the Church. At first the civil tribunals limited the Church's exercise of authority to wills and clauses of wills directly benefiting it. After the Reformation the Church was shorn of every vestige of her former prerogatives. In fact, some countries went so far to the other extreme as to deny the Church all rights of being benefited by wills. This was manifestly unjust and was decried as such by representatives of the Church.[4] In the present legislation Canon 1513 enunciates the strict right of the Church to be the beneficiary of grants, legacies and bequests. The formalities of civil law are to be observed as far as possible.

---

[1] Solmi 1014. Ratzinger 115. Pollock-Maitland II, 312.

[2] C. Tolosanum (1056), can. 9, *Ss. Conc.* XIX, 849. C. Nannetense (1127), Epistola I, *Ss. Conc.* XXI, 353. C. Casselensis (1172), Can. 6, *Ss. Conc.* XXII, 134. C. Tolosanum (1229). can. 16, *Ss. Conc.* XXIII, 198. C. Albiense (1254), can. 37, *Ss. Conc.* XXIII, 842.

[3] St. Matt. XVIII, 16. C. 10, X, *de testamentis et ultimis voluntatibus,* III, 26. *Decreta Concilii Romani,* Tit. XX, cap. 1, p. 46. S. C. C., *Melevitana. Ademptionis legati,* 14 Maii 1887; *Thesaurus,* CXLVI, 231–234. S. C. C., *Bergomen, Pii Legati,* 26 Apr. 1902; *Thesaurus,* CLXI, 395. S. C. C., *Bergomen, Declarationis fiduciae,* 16 Julii 1904; *Thesaurus,* CLXIII, 783. Barbosa, *Collectanea Doctorum in Jus Pontificium Universum,* III, 26, 10. Fagnanus III, 10, 2, 28. Laymann III, Tr. 5, C. 2, n. 4. Solmi, *Storia del Diritto Italiano,* 1014.

[4] Martinus V (in Conc. Constantien.) const. *Inter cunctas,* 22 Febr. 1418, art. 31–33; *Fontes,* n. 43. Pius IX, Ep. encycl., *Quanta cura,* 8 Dec. 1864; *Fontes,* n. 542.

2. Rights of Owners to Bequeath or Devise to the Church.

Canon 1513.

§ 1. Qui ex iure naturae et ecclesiastico libere valet de suis bonis statuere, potest ad causas pias, sive per actum inter vivos sive per actum mortis causa, bona relinquere.

Canon 1513, § 1, enunciates the right of owners to dispose of their property—whether personalty or realty—in favor of the Church if they so desire, provided that there is no restriction of the natural or ecclesiastical law. The natural law suggests, for instance, that parents leave sufficient and suitable means for the needs of their children;[1] while the Church in turn restricts the right of some persons to bequeath or devise property.[2] Those not prevented by the natural or ecclesiastical law are at liberty, despite any ruling of civil law to the contrary, to dispose validly and licitly of their goods.[3] This declaration of the rights of individuals to donate, bequeath or devise property to the Church is in accordance with the earliest legislation.[4] This right has existed in fact from the earliest centuries, for the Church has always received property in this manner; and this same right has been recognized in law by all sovereign states during the greater period of their existence.[5]

Until 321, Catholic churches as such were not permitted in Roman law to be heirs;[6] not that they labored under any legal inheritable incapacity in themselves, but because they were discriminated against by civil rulers. Consequently the Church lost considerable property which had been left to it by the faithful. The Emperors Constantine and Theodosius perçeived the injustice of this, and not only recognized the right of the Church but did all in their power to restore property confiscated during the persecutions.[7] From that time on the Church's right to receive grants and devises was recognized and protected in Roman law.

---

1 Schmalzgrueber III, 26, 1, 7.

2 Can. 583.

3 Laski, *Grammar of Politics*, 134.

4 C. Vasense II (442), c. 4, *Ss. Conc.* VI, 453. C. Aurelianense IV (541), c. 19, *Ss. Conc.* IX, 116. C. Aurelianense V (549), C. 16, *Ss. Conc.* IX, 132. C. Lugdunense II (567) c. 2, *Ss. Conc.* IX, 787.

5 Solmi, *Storia del Diritto Italiano*, 418.

6 *Code Theod.* 16, 2, 4. *Code* 1, 2, 13. St. Ambrosius, *Epistola* 18, n. 13, *Ad Valentinianum*, MPL, XVI, 1017.

7 P. Celestinus, *Epistola XXIII ad Theodosium Juniorem post Synodum Ephesinum*, MPL, L, 546.

From the first centuries the practice of bequeathing property to the Church seems to have been very general. The faithful were anxious to have Masses said for the repose of their souls, to spread the faith by the establishment of monasteries and churches and to help the poor and afflicted by providing annuities and institutions for them. Bequests to the Church were recognized as sure means of accomplishing all this. That this conviction engendered a universal custom of leaving property to the Church is clear from the ever-recurring mention of legacies in favor of the Church;[1] from the frequent admonitions of popes and councils about the conscientious attestation and execution of wills;[2] and from the threats of excommunication against those violating the Church's right to wills.[3]

Whenever the rights of individuals to bequeath to the Church were impugned the Church was bound in the interest of justice and truth to refute the errors as far as possible. Thus the Council of Constance condemned Wycliffe's propositions which held that it was sinful to found convents; that to bequeath money to the clergy was against the teaching of Christ; and that Constantine erred in enriching the Church.[4] Similar errors were branded as contrary to the teaching of Christ and the Church by Pope

---

[1] St. Hieronymus ad Nepotianum, *Epist.* LII, MPL, XXII, 532. *Testamentum Caesaris Arletensis* (508) MPL, LXVII, 1139. *Testamentum Aredii*, MPL LXXI, 1143. *Testamentum Radegundae*, MPL, LXXII, 679. *Testamentum Domoli*, MPL, LXXII, 644. *Testamentum Hadoindi*, MPL, LXXX, 567. *Testamentum Bertichramni*, MPL, LXXX, 587. *Testamentum Tellonis* (766), MPL, XCVI, 1555. *Testamentum Remegii* MPL, XCVI, 1582. *Testamentum Riculfi*, MPL, CXXXII, 468.

Some of the wills cited aim to fulfill requirements of civil law, while others emphasize their adherence to rulings of Canon law. This indicates that during the transitional period from the seventh to the eleventh century, both systems were operating concurrently.

[2] St. Gregorius M. ad Januarium, *Epist.* VIII, Lit. IV, Indict. XII, MPL, LXXVII, 674. St. Gregorius M. ad Januarium, *Epist.* VII, Lit. IX, Indict. II, MPL, LXXVII, 947. St. Gregorius M. ad Januarium, *Epist.* IX, Lit. IV, Indict. XII, MPL, LXXVII, 677. C. Aureliانse IV (541), c. 19, *Ss. Conc.* IX, 116. C. Matisconense I (581), c. 4, *Ss. Conc.* IX, 931. C. 15, C. XVI, q. 1. C. 3, X, *de testamentis et ultimis voluntatibus*, III, 26.

[3] C. 4, 9, C. XIII, q. 2. C. 2, 5, 19, X, *de testamentis et ultimis voluntatibus*, III, 26. C. un., *de testamentis et ultimis voluntatibus*, III, 6 in Clem. C. 2, *de religiosis domibus*, III, 11 in Clem. C. Aurelianense V (549) c. 16, *Ss. Conc.* IX, 132. C. Lugdunense II (567) c. 2, *Ss. Conc.* IX, 787. C. Parisiense V (615) c. 10. *Ss. Conc.* X, 541.

[4] Martinus V (in. Conc. Constantien), const. *Inter cunctas*, 22 Febr. 1418, Fontes n. 43.

Pius IX.[1] Condemnation of such errors is not motivated by any desire to protect bequests because they are a means of enriching the Church. Rather outraged justice demands that the inherent rights of both individual and Church be recognized. The individual owner can dispose of his property in any way he desires provided he does not thereby directly jeopardize the public good. On the other hand the Church has the right of acquiring property by all just means of the natural and positive law,[2] and bequests and legacies are universally acknowledged as legitimate means of acquisition. Moreover the system of bequests and grants is expedient for both Church and individual. By gifts, bequests and endowments the Church is enabled to extend the bounds of its service to mankind, to embellish its temples more fittingly and to carry on its work with greater security. In virtue of these same bequests and legacies, individuals can continue their good works after their decease with the positive assurance that their gifts will be applied as they request; while those who have omitted to fulfill the precept of charity during life can find therein a way of repairing their negligence.[3]

3. Testamentary Formalities Required by Civil Law.

§ 2. In ultimis voluntatibus in bonum Ecclesiae serventur, si fieri possit, sollemnitates iuris civilis; hae si omissae fuerint, heredes moneantur ut testatoris voluntatem adimpleant.

Canon 1513, § 2, urges that, in last wills benefiting the Church, the formalities of civil law be observed if this be possible. This precautionary measure is suggested to facilitate and expedite the probating and filing of testamentary bequests. The Church in no way relinquishes its right to be beneficiary of wills and bequests, but merely wishes to observe the requirements of civil law for convenience and security. No civil legislation, however, could deprive the Church of property to which it has a just right even if the non-essential requirements of law are sometimes lacking.[4] In such cases the Church's right must be respected in

---

[1] Pius IX, ep. encycl. *Quanta cura,* 8 Dec. 1864; Fontes n. 542.

[2] Can. 1499, § 1.

[3] I Prov. Council of Halifax, *Coll. Lacensis* III, 746. I Prov. Council of Westminster (1852), XXV, II, *Coll. Lacensis* III, 942.

[4] H. Laski, *Grammar of Politics,* (London, 1925,) 134.

accordance with the doctrine enunciated by Pope Alexander III.[1] Later legislation has followed the same principles, but the Church has not always rigorously insisted on its full rights.

In 1901 the Sacred Penitentiaria[2] declared that pious bequests are generally valid in the eyes of the Church and considered binding in conscience even if they are held as valid in civil law on account of the omission of formalities. In such cases, however, the Church is not averse to compromise with the heirs so as to avoid litigations and scandals.[3] This decision is virtually incorporated in Canon 1513, § 2, which counsels that the requirements of civil law be observed, if possible, in wills benefiting the Church. If these are omitted the heirs are to be notified and warned of their obligation to fulfill the will of the testator. No further action is necessary, as indiscreet and long-continued insistence would engender difficulties and futile conflicts.

Whenever such cases come to a confessor's attention, he must act very prudently, especially when wills have been declared invalid in the civil courts as lacking the necessary formalities. If the heirs are in good faith or are unwilling to heed the wishes of the testator, since these have been ruled as not binding in law, then the confessor ought to have recourse to the Sacred Penitentiaria for a composition or condonation. Ordinarily this can be easily secured.[4]

The formalities of wills required by the laws of different nations are extremely variant and almost defy brief summary. Even in this country, the divergences are so numerous that the scope of the present work will permit only a cursory mention of the main points of legislation. The forms of testamentary disposition most generally referred to are: written testaments or ordinary wills; nuncupative or oral wills; and holographic wills, which are dated, signed and written in entirety by the testator.[5]

---

[1] C. 11, X, *de testamentis et ultimis voluntatibus*, III, 26.

This decree, it must be admitted, was addressed to the judges of Velletri but according to the common opinion of the theologians its force was in no wise limited to that territory.

Reiffenstuel III, 26, VI, n. 138–147. Schmalzgrueber III, 26, n. 33. D'Annibale II, 339, nota 30.

[2] S. Poenit., 10 Jan. 1901; *Coll.* 2099.

[3] D'Annibale II, 339. Retzbach 13.

[4] Cocchi VI, 372. Vermeersch-Creusen, II, 835. Genicot-Salsmans, I, 675. Noldin II, 520.

[5] In Louisiana there exists a secret or mystic testament which is a will sealed by the testator and so delivered by him to a notary public in the presence of seven witnesses who with the notary write their names on the envelope. *Louisiana Civil Code*, Art. 1584–1588.

Oral Wills.

Oral or nuncupative wills are allowed in some form in all States except Connecticut, Louisiana and Wyoming;[1] but can be made only by soldiers in actual service and mariners at sea in several States;[2] and only by soldiers when in actual service, or mariners at sea, in peril and fear of death, or by anyone in fear of death from an injury received the same day, in certain other States.[3]

To prove oral wills three witnesses are required by some States;[4] in other States there is no provision as to the number of witnesses;[5] while in all other States two witnesses are required. These witnesses must testify that the declaration of the deceased to make a will was made in their joint presence in those States which require that the testamentary intent be proved.[6] Oral wills must then be committed to writing within a certain period after the pronouncement of the words. This period varies from six to sixty days in the different States.[7]

Written Wills.

Written wills, of course, are the more common means of disposing of property. These may be in any language understood by the testator and may be in pencil, print or typewriting.[8] They are to be signed in the handwriting, or equivalently by the mark, of the person devising the property. This signing is usually at

---

[1] Stone's Appeal (1901), 74 Conn. 301, 50 Atl. 734. In Louisiana, the law in relation to nuncupative wills is peculiar to that state. 28 R. C. L. (109) p. 155. 67 A. S. R. 575.

[2] Kentucky, Maryland, Massachusetts, Minnesota, New York, Oregon, Rhode Island, Virginia and West Virginia.

[3] California, Montana, North Dakota, Oklahoma, and South Dakota. Ann. Cas. 1916 A 484.

[4] Arizona, District of Columbia, Florida, Georgia, Maine, Nebraska, New Jersey, New Hampshire, South Carolina, Texas, Wisconsin. 28 R. C. L. p. 158. 26 Am. Dec. 115.

[5] Alabama, Idaho, Maryland, Massachusetts, Minnesota, New York, Oregon, Rhode Island, Vermont, Virginia, West Virginia.

[6] Alabama, Arizona, Arkansas, California, Colorado, Delaware, Florida, Georgia, Illinois, Indiana, Kansas, Kentucky, Maine, Missouri, Montana, Nebraska, Nevada, New Jersey, New Hampshire, North Carolina, North Dakota, Ohio, Oklahoma, Pennsylvania, South Carolina, South Dakota, Texas, Washington and Wisconsin.

[7] 28 R. C. L. 150. 26 Am. Dec. 115.

[8] Myers v. Vanderbelt (1877), 84 Pa. St. 510, 24 Am. Rep. 227. Philbrick v. Spangler (1860), 15 La. An. 46.

the end of the will in conformity with the requirements of most states.

Although seals are frequently attached to wills they are generally unnecessary (except perhaps in Nevada) and do not take the place of the signature. One reason why a seal is not considered equal to signing is that a seal could at this day be easily counterfeited.[1] In most states written wills are to be attested by witnesses but the number of witnesses required differs in various jurisdictions.[2] In a few states[3] holographic wills are valid even though not attested or subscribed by witnesses.[4] A will would not be strictly holographic if any part of it, necessary to render the instrument complete or affecting its meaning, is not in the handwriting of the testator.[5] Hence a typewritten instrument would not be recognized as constituting such a will.[6] The signature is necessary for holographic wills.[7] The date is likewise essential, but it is not necessary that the date given shall be that upon which the paper was in fact written.[8] With the exception of some states[9] it is not necessary that the witnesses learn from the testator that the writing he is executing is his last will. In most states the witnesses are expressly required to sign the will;[10] although it is not necessary that they do so in joint presence except in Louisiana, South Carolina, New Mexico, Utah, Vermont and Wisconsin. In Connecticut, District of Columbia, Georgia, Maine, Massachusetts, New Hampshire, South Carolina, Vermont, three witnesses are required for a will; while in the other states, two are necessary.

Any person of full age, sound mind and free from constraint

---

[1] Burwell v. Corbin, 1 Rand Va., 131, 10 Am. Dec. 494. 28 R. C. L. 110.

[2] 28 R. C. L. 124.

[3] California, Idaho, Louisiana, Montana, North Dakota, Oklahoma, South Dakota, Utah.

[4] Several other states have statutes substantially similar except that the date is not required: Arizona, Arkansas, Kentucky, Mississippi, Nevada, North Carolina, Texas, Tennessee, Virginia, West Virginia.

[5] 104 A. S. R. 26, 20 Ann. Cas. 369.

[6] In re Dreyfus, 175 Cal. 417, 165 Pac. 941.

[7] 140 A. S. R. 29.

[8] In re Vance, 174, Cal. 122, 162 Pac. 103. L. R. A. 1917 C, 479.

[9] Arkansas, California, Idaho, Louisiana, Montana, New Jersey, New York, North Dakota, Oklahoma, South Dakota, Utah.

[10] Some states have specific statutes requiring the signature to be at the end of the will. The statutes of all the states except Arkansas, Iowa, New York, and Wyoming require the witnesses to sign in the presence of the testator.

may devise or bequeath his property by will,[1] provided substantial error, fraud and undue influence are absent. On the other hand a devise or bequest may be made to any person unless forbidden by express statute, opposed to good morals or contrary to public policy.

The beneficiary of a devise or bequest cannot be left uncertain. For this reason many bequests in trust for Masses have been held void because of the uncertainty of the object and the lack of a person entitled to the benefit of the trust to appeal to the services of the court.[2]

The application of the English charity doctrine to bequests for Masses in American law has given rise to a complex problem as evidenced by the divergent statutes of states and the variant opinions of courts and jurists. In Maryland, Virginia, West Virginia, Michigan, New York, Wisconsin, Minnesota and Mississippi bequests for Masses have been declared void because of the indefiniteness of their beneficiaries.[3] Despite the adverse legislation in these states, gifts for Masses could not be uniformly voided. The courts were generally cognizant of their responsibilities in settling wills according to the intention of the testator, and by an equitable interpretation of the statutes upheld most bequests for Masses.[4] Thus in some cases the courts considered a bequest for Masses as creating a valid private trust;[5] in other instances it was declared that such a bequest lacked perpetuity and the essential elements of a charitable use so as to escape the mortmain statute;[6] or again the bequest was construed as a direct gift to the priest with advisory and precatory phrases to emphasize the serious obligation of performing the sacred services as requested.[7] Because of the complexities and difficulties of our laws on the question of charities great care should be exercised in

[1] Swinburne, *Wills*, Book 1, part 2.

[2] Festorazzi v. St. Joseph's Catholic Church of Mobile (1894), 104 Ala. 327, 18, So. 394, L. R. A. 360. Shanahan v. Kelly (1903), 88, Minn. 92 N. W. 948. McHugh v. McCole (1897), 97 Wis. 166, 72 N. W. 631, 65 Am. St. Rep. 106, 40 L. R. A. 724.

[3] New York, Michigan, and Wisconsin have revised their laws so as to uphold bequests for Masses.

[4] Holland v. Smyth (1886) 3 How. Prac. (N. S.) 106, 109. In re Zimmerman, (1890) 50 N. Y. Supp. 395, 22 Misc. Rep. 411. Zollmann, *American Law of Charities*, 179.

[5] Moran v. Moran, (1897), 104 Iowa 216, 225; 73 N. W. 617, 39 L. R. A. 204; 65 Am. St. Rep. 443.

[6] In re Lannon (1907) 152 Cal. 327, 330; 92 Pac. 870; Am. St. Rep. 58.

[7] Harrison v. Brophy, 59 Kans. 1, 51 Pac. 883; 40 L. R. A. 721.

making any devises to the Church and especially in establishing bequests for Masses. Such gifts are recognized as valid charities in American law but can be easily contested if not properly made.[1]

Despite the fact that bequests for Masses were void in many instances in this country, they were never invalidated under the plea of "superstitious uses," as was the case for many centuries in England.[2] These statutes of English law were never incorporated in American law even though they left a marked impression on our jurisprudence.[3] In 1531 a statute against "superstitious uses," aimed directly at the Church, was passed in England.[4] The aims of the state religion, recognized and established by law in England after the Reformation, were deemed to be pious; whereas the purposes of all other religions and particularly the Catholic were held as superstitious.

In this country such discriminations were not legally possible;[5] for there is no established religion and the Government cannot actively participate in the support or dissemination of religion of any sort to the discrimination of another. Hence a bequest for the celebration of Masses cannot be held void as giving effect to the religious superstitions of donors. The validity of such a bequest is to be treated on the same principle that would be applied to a devise in aid of religious observances of any denomination, inasmuch as American courts have nothing to do with creeds or their orthodoxy.[6] There is, it is true, diversity of opinion as to the execution of such bequests but they are generally held to be valid.[7] According to decisions handed down, the saying of Mass by a priest is considered a ceremonial open to all who choose to be present; a solemn and impressive ritual form from which many draw spiritual solace, guidance and instruction. While the effect of such service upon the members

[1] Zollmann, *American Law of Charities*, 180.

[2] Bequests for Masses are now considered valid in England, *Eccles. Review*, LXII, (1920) 646.

[3] Desmond, *Church and Law*, 49.

[4] 1, Edward VI, c. 14. 3, William IV, c. 115. Pitts v. James, 1 Rolle 416. Harrison v. Brophy, 59 Kan. 1, 51 Pac. 883, 40 L. R. A. 721. Holland v. Alcock, 108 N. Y. 312, 16 N. E. 305, 2 A. S. R. 420. Sherman v. Baker, 20 R. I. 446, 40 Atl. 11, 40 L. R. A. 717.

[5] Hoeffer v. Clogan (1898), 171 Ill. 462, 49 N. E. 527, 40 L. R. A. 730.

[6] Festorazzi v. St. Joseph's Cath. Church of Mobile, 104 Ala. 327, 53 A. S. R. 48. McHugh v. McCole, 97 Wis. 166, 72 N. W. 631, 65 A. S. R. 106. Kavanaugh v. Watt, 143 Wis. 90, 126 N. W. 672, 28 L. R. A. (N. S.) 470.

[7] Sherman v. Baker, 20 R. I. 466, 40 Atl. 11, 40 L. R. A. 717.

of the Church is impressive and beneficial the money expended for the celebration of Mass is of benefit to the clergy; and such a trust is to be upheld and maintained for this reason as one of the cherished objects of religious uses.[1] Both the federal and most state constitutions contain provisions of guarantee of religious liberty to all denominations and the courts have always upheld the doctrine of religious toleration.[2]

Two other important points of law in connection with wills in favor of the Church are: that some states limit the amount of one's property that may be given to charity;[3] while there are also laws that make testamentary gifts to charity void if they are executed within a certain period of the testator's death.[4] The purpose of the former limitation is to check the generosity of donors to the impoverishment of their children or relatives; while the aim of the latter is "to prohibit a testator, unless the act is accompanied with due deliberation, and unless such time is allowed to elapse as gives an opportunity to revoke the same, if hasty or ill-considered, from setting aside the claims of those whom he is leaving behind him."[5]

Construction of Wills.

The correct construction of wills is a very perplexing problem as Lord Coke sagely observed more than two centuries ago.[6] "With the desire to reduce to a minimum the perplexity and uncertainty inseparable from the subject, the courts have established certain more or less artificial and arbitrary canons of construction, by which certain forms of expression are presumed to have certain meanings, and in doubtful cases these presump-

---

[1] Hoeffer v. Clogan, 171 Ill. 462, 49 N. E. 527, 63 A. S. R. 241, 40 L. R. A. 730.

[2] Coleman v. O'Leary (1902), 114 Ky. 388, 401, 402; 24 Ky. L. Rep. 1248; S. W. 1068. Harrison v. Brophy (1898) 59 Kan. 1, 5, 51; Pac. 883; 40 L. R. A. 721. In re Kavanaugh (1910) 143 Wis. 90, 96; 126 N. W. 672. Breen v. Allen (1844) 24 Tenn. (5 Humph) 170, 188. *Amer. Eccles. Review*, XX, 1899, 162; LXII, (1920) 646; LXII, (1920), 289.

[3] St. John v. Andrew Institute (1907), 191 N. Y. 254, 275, 83 N. E. 981. McLean v. Wade (1861), 41 Pa. 266, 269. Kerr v. Dougherty (1878), 59 How. Prac. 44; affirmed 79 N. Y. 327.

[4] Downing v. Marshall (1861), 23 N. Y. 366, 387; Am. Dec. 290. Stephenson v. Short, (1883) 92 N. Y. 433, 440.

[5] Kerr v. Dougherty (1878) 59 How, Prac. 44, 58; Affirmed 79, N. Y. 327.

[6] Keteltas v. Keteltas, 72 N. Y. 312, 28 Am. Rep. 155, 12 L. R. A. (N. S.) 283.

tions are held to be decisive."[1] Because of the difficulty of constructing a will correctly persons versed in the technicalities of law should usually be consulted in the making of wills benefiting the Church in any way. "All rules of construction are designed to ascertain and give effect to the intention of the testator, for the purpose of the construction of a will is to ascertain the intention of the testator as expressed in the will, viewed in the light of the attending circumstances."[2]

In the United States the laws of the different states vary appreciably in the matter of the proper construction of wills. Hence all parties interested should consult lawyers when making wills in favor of the Church.[3]

4. Fulfilment and Execution of Wills.

Canon 1514.

Voluntates fidelium facultates suas in pias causas donantium vel relinquentium, sive per actum inter vivos, sive per actum mortis causa, diligentissime impleantur etiam circa modum administrationis et erogationis bonorum, salvo praescripto can. 1515, § 3.

The Church has always regarded the fulfilment of the stipulations of wills as a sacred obligation. Canon 1514 but restates the legislation of centuries, formulated even in Roman law,[4] and ever strictly observed in Canon law.[5] Decretal law is very insistent that the intention of devisors be conscientiously fulfilled. Thus Gregory IX empowered bishops to see to the fulfilment of the wills that were not properly executed within one year;[6] and even to interdict the goods of those who violated wills.[7] Trustees and executors were to be constrained to fulfill wills favoring pious works in accordance with the intention of the donors;[8] if executors—even religious—failed to execute wills

[1] 28 R. C. L. 204. In re Paxson, 241 Pa. St. 452, 88 Atl. 673, L. R. A. 1915, C. 1009.

[2] 28 R. C. L. 204. Andrews v. Applegate, 223 Ill, 535, 79 N. E. 176, 7 Ann. Cas. 126, 12 L. R. A. (N. S.) 661. McDermott v. Scully, 91 Conn. 45, 98 Atl. 350, Ann. Cas. 1917 E. 407.

[3] Technically correct forms will be found in Zollmann's scholarly work, *American Law on Charities*, Milwaukee, 1924.

[4] *Code*, 1, 2, 14, 1; 1, 2, 22; 1, 3, 45 pr. *Novellae* 131, 11.

[5] C. 4, 11, C. XIII, q. 2. C. 15, C. XVI, q. 1. C. 4, C. XVII, q. 4.

[6] C. 3, X, *de testamentis et ultimis voluntatibus*, III, 26.

[7] C. 6, X, *de testamentis et ultimis voluntatibus*, III, 26.

[8] C. 17, X, *de testamentis et ultimis voluntatibus*, III, 26.

conscientiously they were to be punished;[1] and those who violated sacred trusts were to be severely reprehended.[2]

The Council of Trent, in restating the Constitution "Quia contingit" of the Council of Vienne,[3] is equally emphatic that institutions founded by wills and bequests should be conscientiously managed.[4] Later doctrine on wills has been even stricter about the fulfilment of the intentions of devisors and the clauses of wills,[5] as is evident from the decisions of the S. Congregation of the Council.[6] This is necessary, for in accepting wills, the Church secures an inviolable trust and assumes a sacred obligation.[7] Moreover, devisors have a right to expect that their intentions will be carried out as far as is humanly possible;[8] while the faithful would be justly scandalized if the express wishes of the dead were disregarded.[9] So insistent is the Church upon the fulfilment of pious legacies and wills that Canon 2348 empowers Ordinaries to coerce, even by censure, those who neglect the fulfilment of testamentary bequests even if these are held only in trust. In the execution of wills special attention must be paid to the clauses of the document and the intention of the devisor. These must be conformed to as closely as possible.[10]

The difficulty of fulfilling all the bequests of testators is evi-

---

[1] C. un., *de testamentis et ultimis voluntatibus*, III, 6 in Clem.

[2] C. 2, *de religiosis domibus*, III, 11 in Clem.

[3] C. 2, *De religiosis domibus*, III, 11 in Clem.

[4] Sess. VII, *de ref.*, c. 15.

[5] Benedictus XIV, const. *Ad militantis*, 30 Martii 1742, 30, 31 *Fontes*, n. 326.

[6] S. C. C., *Albanen.*, *Juris patronatus*, 22 Martii 1873; *Thesaurus*, CXXXII (1873), 294. S. C. C., *Bononien.*, *Legati*, 27 Febr. 1875; *Thesaurus*, CXXXIV (1875) 218. S. C. C., *Ravennaten.*, *Commutationis voluntatis*, 31 Jan. 1880; *Thesaurus*, CXXXIX (1880) 58. S. C. C., *Bononien.*, *Legati*, 11 Dec. 1880; *Thesaurus*, CXXXIX (1880) 675. S. C. C., *Romana*, *Beneplaciti*, 12 Martii 1881; *Thesaurus*, CXL (1881) 226. S. C. C., *Bellunen.*, *Exonerationis*, 29 Maii 1886; *Thesaurus*, CXLV (1886) 455. S. C. C., *Andrien.*, *Reductionis onerum*, 24 Julii 1886; *Thesaurus*, CXLV (1886) 692. S. C. C., *Firmana*, *Impositionis oneris*, 2 Aprilis 1887; *Thesaurus*, CXLVI (1887) 164. S. C. C., *Compostellana*, *Validitatis decreti*, 23 Martii 1889; *Thesaurus*, CXLVIII (1889) 389. S. C. C., *Theanen.*, *Adjudicationis redituum*, 15 Junii 1889; *Thesaurus*, CXLVIII (1889) 524. S. C. C., *Vincentina*, *Administrationis*, 14 Dec. 1889; *Thesaurus*, CXLVIII (1889) 928.

[7] Benedictus XIV, const. *Ad. militantis*, 30 Martii 1742; 30, 31, *Fontes*, n. 326.

[8] S. C. C., *Romana*, *Beneplaciti*, 12 Martii 1881; *Thesaurus*, CXL (1881) 226.

[9] S. C. C., *Compostellana*, *Validitatis decreti*, 23 Martii 1889; *Thesaurus*, CXLVIII (1889) 389.

[10] Reiffenstuel III, 26, 23, n. 800–804.

dent from the application of what is known as the "cy pres" doctrine in English and American law. This doctrine is frequently applied as a means of sustaining gifts to charities that might otherwise lapse. The meaning of the doctrine is that when a definite function or duty is to be performed and it cannot be done in exact conformity with the scheme of the testator, it must be performed with as close an approximation to that scheme as is reasonably practicable. It follows from the principle that where there is a general and particular intent and the particular one is rendered ineffectual, the phraseoloby is to be so construed as to give effect to the general intent.[1] This is done lest the intent of the donor fail of accomplishment.[2] The most liberal judicial rules are therefore applied so as to realize to some extent the will of the testator,[3] and generally every presumption consistent with the language employed will be allowed.[4]

Canon 1515.

§ 1. Ordinarii omnium piarum voluntatum tam mortis causa quam inter vivos exsecutores sunt.

§ 2. Hoc ex iure Ordinarii vigilare possunt, ac debent, etiam per visitationem, ut piae voluntates impleantur, et alii exsecutores delegati debent, perfuncti munere, illis reddere rationem.

§ 3. Clausulae huic Ordinariorum iuri contrariae, ultimis voluntatibus adiectae, tanquam non appositae habeantur.

In conformity with the provisions of Justinianean law,[5] and the Canons of the Church[6] the Code declares Ordinaries to be the executors of all pious gifts whether these be by simple donation or last will.[7] Canon 1515 substantially restates the doctrine of

---

[1] Teele v. Derry, 168 Mass. 341, 47 N. E. 422, 60 A. S. R. 401, 38 L. R. A. 629. Philadelphia v. Girard, 45 Pa. St. 9, 84 Am. Dec. 470. Edgerly v. Barker, 66 N. H. 434, 31 Atl. 900, 28 L. R. A. 328.

[2] Harrington v. Pier, 105 Wis. 485, 82 N. W. 345, 76 A. S. R. 924, 50 L. R. A. 307.

[3] Maxcy v. Oshkosh, 144 Wis., 238, 128 N. W. 899, 31 L. R. A. (N. S.) 787.

[4] Franklin v. Hastings, 253 Ill. 46, 97 N. E. 265, Ann. Cas. A. 135.

[5] *Code*, 1, 3, 45.

[6] C. 3, 6, 17, X, *de testamentis et ultimis voluntatibus*, III, 26. C. un. *de testamentis et ultimus voluntatibus*, III, 6 in Clem. S. C. C., *Pinnen, Legatorum*, 29 Aprilis 1871; *Thesaurus*, CXXX (1871) 423.

[7] Fagnanus III, 3, 9. Barbosa, *Collectanea Doctorum in Jus Pontificium Universum*, III, 26, c. 17.

the Council of Trent,[1] even though there are a few significant changes. It is to be noted that the Code employs the word "Ordinarius" instead of "Episcopi," the term of the Council. This is intentional so as to include Vicars and Prefects Apostolic as well as higher superiors of clerical exempt religious institutes.[2] Furthermore the Code omits two clauses: "etiam tamquam sedis apostolicae delegati" and "in casibus a jure concessis," connoting that the scope of the Ordinaries' power has been extended.

Since the Ordinaries are constituted the executors of all wills within their jurisdiction it is incumbent upon them, either personally or through competent delegates, to see that these are properly executed in accordance with Canon 1515, § 2. In cases where special executors are appointed, Ordinaries must keep themselves informed as to the care with which the work of execution is discharged. If necessary, visitations should be made to this effect even to institutes otherwise exempt from episcopal visitation.[3]

Clauses in wills contrary to the Ordinaries' rights as executors are to be considered as non-existent. This provision originated in Justinianean law[4] and has been retained and observed in canonical legislation since.[5]

---

[1] Sess. XII, *de ref.*, c. 8: "Episcopi, etiam tamquam sedis apostolicae delegati, in casibus a jure concessis omnium piarum dispositionum tam in ultima voluntate quam inter vivos sint exsecutores."

[2] Can. 198, §1. Blat, (in h. can., p. 517) in opposition to the wording of the Canon and the weight of the best authorities (Vermeersch–Creusen, II, n. 836; Pruemmer, 525; Augustine, VI, 572) is of the opinion that higher superiors of exempt religious institutes are to be excluded by the nature of the matter in question: "Hi excluduntur evidenter ob naturam rei de qua agitur, scilicet donationes laicorum vel clericorum bona possidentium, ac inde religiosorum." However, as is clear from the Canon the matter need not necessarily be restricted to the gifts of laics. Hence, Pruemmer (1 c.) more correctly remarks: "Ordinarii, i. e. episcopi eorumque vicegerentes, si agitur de piis voluntatibus factis pro causis ipsorum jurisdictioni subiectis, et superiores maiores religiosi exempti, si agitur de bonis datis pro ipsorum religione, sunt exsecutores omnium piarum voluntatum."

[3] A. S. S. II, 369, Appendix X, *Circa officium judicis ecclesiastici in exsecutione piarum voluntatum seu dispositionum.* Fagnanus, in C. 2, *de relig. domibus,* III, 11 in Clem., n. 7–10. De Luca, *De jurisdictione et foro competenti,* III, Disc. 40, n. 14. Vermeersch-Creusen II, n. 836.

[4] *Code* 1, 3, 45.

[5] C. 17, X, *de testamentis et ultimis voluntatibus,* III, 26. S. C. C., *Pinnen., Legatorum,* 29 Aprilis 1870; *Thesaurus,* CXXX (1871) 423. Lugo, *De justitia et jure,* Disp. 24, n. 337.

5. Clerics and Religious as Trustees.

Canon 1516.

§ 1. Clericus vel religiosus qui bona ad pias causas sive per actum inter vivos, sive ex testamento fiduciarie accepit, debet de sua fiducia Ordinarium certiorem reddere, eique omnia istiusmodi bona seu mobilia seu immobilia cum oneribus adiunctis indicare; quod si donator id expresse et omnino prohibuerit, fiduciam ne acceptet.

§ 2. Ordinarius debet exigere ut bona fiduciaria in tuto collocentur et vigilare pro exsecutione piae voluntatis ad normam can. 1515.

§ 3. Bonis fiduciariis alicui religioso commissis, si quidem bona sint attributa loci seu dioecesis ecclesiis, incolis aut piis causis iuvandis, Ordinarius de quo in §§ 1, 2, est loci Ordinarius; secus, est Ordinarius eiusdem religiosi proprius.

Canon 1516, § 1, obliges clerics and religious who receive property in trust for pious works to acquaint the Ordinary of the nature of the trust in a detailed report. This Canon is taken substantially from the reply of the S. Congregation of the Council to the Bishop of Beauvais which stated: "Omnes, sive sacerdotes sive laicos, quorum fidei concredita sunt legata ad pias causas, teneri de hoc quam primum certiorem reddere Episcopum, qui ius habet vigilandi super administrationem et consulendi securitati eorumdem legatorum."[1] The terminology of the Canon differs somewhat from the reply of the S. Congregation. These changes are intentional and significant. The Code, it will be noted, employs the words "clericus vel religiosus" instead of "omnes, sive sacerdotes sive laicos" thus seemingly excluding laics; although laics are not thereby exempt from all obligations.[2] The Code has also omitted the word "quamprimum," presumably for a good reason. The application of the reply of the S. Congregation was more limited as it considered only "legata ad pias causas;" while the Code includes "bona ad pias causas sive per actum inter vivos, sive ex testamento fiduciarie."[3] The determination of the Ordinary to whom the report was to be submitted was not sufficiently clear in the reply to the Bishop of Beauvais,[4] whereas Canon 1516, § 3, clarifies

[1] S. C. C., *Bellovacensis*, 9 Aug. 1909; A. A. S. I, 766.
[2] Vermeersch-Creusen II, n. 836. Blat 519.
[3] *Commentarium pro reli nosis*, III (1922), 266.
[4] Vermeersch, *Periodicu*, V, 51.

this matter. Moreover, the report to the Ordinary, according to the Code, must make mention of all the property—movable or immovable—with all the obligations attached thereto, while this was not specifically required in the previous legislation. Finally, a trust may not be accepted if the devisor of the property expressly forbids the fulfilment of the requirements of Canon 1516, § 1. No such provision was contained in the reply of the S. Congregation.

Canon 1516, § 2, corresponds in a marked degree to the second part of the reply to the Bishop of Beauvais, viz.: "qui ius habet vigilandi super administrationem et consulendi securitati eorumdem legatorum." With greater precision the Canon obliges the Ordinary to require that the object of trust be placed in safe securities. Real estate, governmental and other securely placed bonds are considered safe investments.

In cases where property is left in trust to a religious, the Ordinary bound by the rulings of Canon 1516, §§ 1, 2, will be the "Ordinarius loci" when the objects of trust are given to aid churches (Can. 1161), subjects (Can. 94) or pious works of the place or diocese (215, § 2); in other cases the Ordinary will be the proper Ordinary of the religious. If the religious is a member of a clerical exempt institute his higher superior will be his proper Ordinary; whereas the local Ordinary will be the proper Ordinary in the case of other religious.[1] This Canon implies that a religious may act as a trustee. In individual cases the Constitutions of the different religious organizations should be consulted to ascertain whether the particular Order or Congregation forbids it, as is the case in the Order of Friars Minor.[2]

6. Modification of Wills.

Canon 1517.

§ 1. Ultimarum voluntatum reductio, moderatio, commutatio, quae fieri ex iusta tantum et necessaria causa debent, Sedi Apostolicae reservantur, nisi fundator hanc potestatem etiam Ordinario loci expresse concesserit.

§ 2. Si tamen exsecutio onerum impositorum, ob imminutos reditus aliamve causam, nulla administratorum culpa, impossibilis evaserit, tunc Ordinarius quoque, auditis iis

---

[1] *Commentarium pro religiosis*, III, (1922), 266–269.

[2] *Regula et Constitutiones Generales Fratrum Minorum*, (Quaracchi, 1922) Cap. IV, n. 234. Woywod II, 177.

quorum interest, et servata, meliore quo fieri potest modo, fundatoris voluntate, poterit eadem onera aeque imminuere, excepta Missarum reductione quae semper Sedi Apostolicae unice competit.

The dictates of conscience and positive laws postulate that the intentions of testators and creators of trusts be fulfilled with exactitude. This is generally easy of attainment within a few years or even a generation of the devisor's death. But as the years and centuries wear on social and financial changes arise; the mutations of time may witness territorial changes of great importance. Cataclysms of vast extent may disrupt empires and change institutions so that a modification of a will may become imperative at times. To allow wills to be changed without sufficient reason would tend to destroy faith in the stability of testamentary systems;[1] while a refusal of reasonable changes or commutations for just and necessary reasons would work untold hardships upon individuals and sometimes even militate against public good.[2] Hence the Church, founding its legislation upon the principles of Roman law[3] and later enunciating its own distinctive statutes—endued with the wisdom of century-long experience—has formulated the ruling of Canon 1517, § 1, which allows the reduction, change or commutation of wills only for just and necessary reasons. And this power is reserved to the Holy See, unless the founder has expressly conceded it to the local Ordinary.

The early legislation in this matter is not precise nor clear, but it indicates that the provisions of all wills were conscientiously observed.[4] The Council of Trent enacted a definite law that the alterations of last wills—possible only for just and necessary reasons—were not to be allowed until the bishops, acting as delegates of the Apostolic See, had verified the petitions lest truth be suppressed and falsehood suggested.[5] This law was

---

[1] S. C. C., *Romana, Beneplaciti,* 12 Martii 1881; *Thesaurus,* CXL (1880) 226. S. C. C., *Compostellana, Validitatis decreti,* 23 Martii 1889; *Thesaurus,* CXLVIII (1889), 389.

[2] *Annals of American Academy of Political and Social Science,* Sept. 1925, CXXI, 210.

[3] *Digest* 33, 2, 16.

[4] St. Gregorius Magnus, *Epistola* IX, IV, XII; MPL, LXXVII, 677. C. 14, C. XVI, q. 1. C. 2. *de religiosis domibus,* III, 11 in Clem.

[5] Sess., XXII, *de ref.,* III, c. 6.

consistently observed as evinced in later decisions[1] and writings of noted canonists.[2]

An Instruction of S. C. of Propaganda in 1807[3] is a clear exposition of the legislation and shows how the exercise of power of commuting wills was restricted directly to the Holy See. In this Instruction, general faculties for commuting pious legacies and offerings were refused. Instead a decree was issued[4] authorizing the Apostolic Vicar of Cochin—because of the great distance and slow means of travel and communication—to commute these only in cases of necessity and when the fulfilment of the prescribed works became impossible. Moreover, this commutation was to be made "in opera meliora" and with the consent of the missionaries with the final requirement that it was to be transmitted to the S. C. of Propaganda for approval.

Canon 1517, § 1, makes it clear that in conformity with the old legislation, just and necessary causes are required for the reduction, change or commutation of last wills and that this power is regularly reserved to the Holy See.[5] If the founder expressly authorizes the local Ordinary to moderate or change the provisions of the will, the agency of the Holy See is not necessary. In such a case the will would not really be changed but the provisory clause empowering the Bishop to act would merely be called into force.

At times the fulfilment of the obligations imposed by last wills may become impossible because of decreased revenues or

[1] S. C. C., *Isernien.*, 5 Sept. et 14 Nov. 1705; Richter, *Canones et Decreta Concilii Tridentini*, 161. S. C. C., *Arianen.*, 7 Febr. 1733; Richter, *Canones et Decreta Concilii Tridentini*, 161. S. C. C., *Montis Politani*, 19 Aug. 1724; Richter 162. S. C. C., *Fulginaten.*, 20 Nov. et 4 Dec. 1762; Richter 162. S. C. C., *Cathacen.*, 18 Nov. 1719; Richter 163. S. C. C., *Romana*, 27 Febr. 1734; Richter 164. S. C. C., *Aretina*, 21 Julii 1742; Richter 165. S. C. C., *Pinnen.*, *Legatorum*, 29 Aprilis 1870; *Thesaurus*, CXXX (1870) 435. S. C. C., *Montisfalisci*, *Cappellanicae*, 26 Julii 1873; *Thesaurus*, CXXXII (1870) 586. S. C. C., *Ravennaten.*, *Commutationis voluntatis*, 31 Jan. 1880; *Thesaurus*, CXXXIX (1880) 58. S. C. C., *Galtellinoren.*, *Adscriptionis bonorum*, 19 Maii 1888; *Thesaurus*, CXLVII (1888) 341. S. C. C., *Vincentina*, *Administrationis*, 14 Dec. 1889; *Thesaurus*, CXLVIII (1889) 928. S. C. C., *Compostellana*, *Validitatis decreti*, 23 Martii 1889; *Thesaurus*, CXLVIII (1889) 389. S. C. C., *Calaritana*, *Jurium*, 26 Junii 1897; *Thesaurus*, CLVI (1897) 676.

[2] Benedictus XIV, *De synodo dioecesana*, Lib. XIII, c. ult. De Luca, *De testamentis*, Disc. 72, n. 14. Moneta, *De commutatione ultimum conclusionum*, I, n. 18. Barbosa, *De officio ac potestate episcopi*, P. III, Alleg. 83.

[3] *Coll.* n. 689.

[4] S. C. Prop. Fide, 25 Jan. 1807; *Coll.* n. 689.

[5] S. C. C., *Commutationis voluntatis*, 27 Junii 1863; A. S. S. I, 608. Lugo, *De justitia et jure*, Disp. XXIV, Sect. 13, n. 312. Sebastianelli II, 337.

other reasons. If this is due to no fault of the administrators, the Ordinary may diminish the burdens equitably after consulting all interested parties. Such cases can become especially numerous after national and international crises like the World War, when money values depreciate and economic orders are upset.[1] In reducing the burdens of wills under such circumstances the Ordinaries should exercise the greatest discretion and ought to try to discern, as closely as possible, the likely intention of the founder. Cases decided by the S. C. of the Council should furnish the norms for the guidance of Ordinaries in this important matter.

In conformity with the ruling of the Constitution "Nuper" of Innocent XII,[2] the Holy See regularly reserves to itself the right to reduce Mass obligations.[3] The legislation of the Council of Trent was less strict in this matter.[4] It empowered bishops in diocesan synods as well as abbots and generals of Orders in their general chapters to make the regulations they deemed expedient for diminishing the obligations of Masses. This concession of power was abused and the constitution of Innocent XII with its severe legislation followed as a necessary consequence. The Code has seen fit to retain this legislation out of reverence for the rights of donors and as a safeguard against abuses. The Roman Congregations competent in this matter are:—in the external forum: The S. Congregation of the Council, the Fabric of St. Peter's, the S. Congregation of Propaganda for mission countries and the S. Congregation of Religious;[5] in the internal forum: the S. Penitentiaria. These Congregations oftentimes delegate faculties to Ordinaries for diminishing the obligations of foundations in accordance with the stipends of the time. Masses of foundation are understood from the context; but the

---

[1] Pruemmer 526. Cocchi VI, 377.

[2] 23 Dec. 1697, §§ 3, 15, *Fontes* n. 260.

[3] S. C. C., *Albanus, Cessationis onerum Missarum*, 30 Ian. 1846, Bizzarri, 531. S. C. C., *Congregationis Passionis*, 16 Dec. 1893, ASS. XXVI, 397. D'Annibale III, 74–76. For faculties granted to Nuncios and Apostolic Delegates in this matter consult Vermeersch-Cruesen I, Appendix 1, n. 715; Woywod, Appendix IV, 638, n. 6; *Il Monitore Ecclesiastico* XVIII (1906), 34; XXIX (1917), 77–91.

[4] Sess. XXV, *de ref.*, c. 4.

[5] In all likelihood the Consistorial Congregation is competent in this regard concerning the "mensa episcopalis" and the S. Congregation of Seminaries and Universities for institutions under its control. Vermeersch-Cruesen II, n. 836; *Periodica* XII, 43.

ruling of this Canon would apply with even greater force to manual Masses.

The Pontifical Commission for the authentic interpretation of the Code[1] makes clear the powers of Ordinaries in virtue of the present Canon. As was to be expected, the reply stated that if the document or the charter of foundation expressly gives him the right the Ordinary can reduce Mass obligations. In wills containing such provisory clauses the intention of the founder is that the Ordinaries be empowered to reduce the obligations under certain conditions. The conditions being fulfilled the Ordinaries are acting the part of executors and hence need no special authorization of the Holy See.

---

[1] 14 Julii 1922; A. A. S. XIV, 529; *Periodica* XI, 165.

CONCLUSION.

The rulings of Canon law on the acquisition of property and ecclesiastical goods clearly show how minutely the Church wishes to regulate all matters of great moment. The Catholic Church has an innate, lawful and inalienable right to acquire property by all just means allowed to others. This property is devoted to God and is used directly or indirectly in His service. Hence the great care which the Church must use in the acquisition of such goods so that the sacred dictates of charity and justice be duly observed. The means of acquiring ecclesiastical property are various. Canon Law, founded on the experience of ages, legislates in regard to these means not that the acquisitive powers of the Church might thereby work the more efficiently and potently; but that neither the rights of the Church nor those of the individual be violated. The Church stands for justice. It has a right to acquire property which no nation can impugn or legislate away; it has its own statutes so that no rash exactions be made from its members; it has its rules for prescription and its formalities for the acceptance of donations and legacies; in a word, with supreme and ripe wisdom, it aims in its legislation in this matter as in all things else to tend toward its own end: the salvation of souls and the furtherance of God's work on earth.

BIBLIOGRAPHIA

I. FONTES IURIDICI.

AAS = *Acta Apostolicae Sedis*, Romae, 1909—.
ASS = *Acta Sanctae Sedis*, 41 vol., Romae, 1865–1908.
Acta et Decreta Sacrorum Conciliorum Recentiorum (Collectio Lacensis), 5 vol., Friburgi Brisgoviae, 1870–1879.
Acta Ecclesiae Mediolanensis, Mediolani, 1599.
Acta et Decreta Concilii Plenarii Baltimorensis II, 1868.
Acta et Decreta Concilii Plenarii Baltimorensis III, 1886.
Acta et Decreta Concilii Plenarii Americae Latinae, Romae, 1900.
Basilicorum Libri LX, 6 vol., ed., G. G. E. Heimbach, Lipsiae, 1833.
Canones et Decreta Concilii Tridentini—ed., F. Schulte et A. L. Richter, Lipsiae, 1853.
Causae Selectae in S. C. Cardinal. Conc. Trident. Interp. Propositae, S. Lingen et P. A. Reuss, Ratisboniae, 1871.
Codex Iuris Canonici Pii X Pontificis Maximi iussu digestus Benedicti Papae XV auctoritate promulgatus, Romae, 1917.
Code = *Codex Iustinianus*, recognovit et retractavit Paulus Krueger, Vol. II *Corporis Iuris Civilis*, Berolini, 1915.
Code Theod. = *Theodosiani Libri XVI cum Constitutionibus Sirmondianus et Leges Novellae ad Theodosianum Pertinentes*, ed. P. Krueger, Th. Mommsen, P. M. Meyer, 3 vol., Berolini, 1905.
Coll. = *Collectanea S. Congregationis de Propaganda Fide*, 2 vol., 1907.
Collectanea in Usum Secretariae Sacrae Congregationis Episcoporum et Regularium Edita (Bizzarri), Romae, 1885.
Corpus Iuris Canonici, Editio Lipsiensis secunda, A. L. Richter et A. Friedberg, 2 vol., Lipsiae, 1922.
Corpus Iuris Civilis; Inst. = *Institutiones*, recognovit P. Krueger; *Dig.* = *Digesta*, recognovit Th. Mommsen, retractavit P. Krueger, Vol. I, Berolini, 1922; *Code* vel C. = *Codex Iustinanus*, recognovit et retractavit P. Krueger, Vol. II, Berolini, 1915; *Nov.* = *Novellae*, recognovit R. Schoell, absolvit G. Kroll, Vol. III, Berolini, 1912.
Corpus Scriptorum Ecclesiasticorum Latinorum, 60 vol., Vindobonae, 1866–1913.
Decreta Concilii Romani (1725), Romae, 1751.
Fontes = *Fontes Codicis Iuris Canonici cura Emil P. Gasparri editi*, 4 vol., Romae, 1923–1926.
Fontes Iuris Romani Anteiustiniani, S. Riccobono, Florentiae, 1909.
Gai Institutiones, ed. E. Poste et E. A. Whittuck, Oxford, 1904.
Institutionum Iuris Civilis Commentaria, V. Saccus, Venetiis, 1774.
Institutionum Libri Quatuor, A. Vinnius, Venetiis, 1758.
Ius Pontificium de Propaganda Fide, 6 vol., J. Card. Simeoni, R. De Martinio, Romae, 1888–1895.
La Sovranita Temporale Di Romani Pontifici propugnata nelle sua integrita dal Suffragio Dell' Orbe Cattolico, 16 vol., Roma, 1860.

Manuale delle Fonti del Diritto Romano secundo i resultati della piu recente critica filogica e giuridica,—cura di P. Cogliolo, 2 ed., Torino, 1911.

Manuale Latinitatis Fontium Iuris Civilis Romanorum, H. E. Dirksen, Berolini, 1837.

S. Conc. = *Sacrorum Conciliorum Nova et Amplissima Collectio* (J. D. Mansi), 51 vol., Florentiae, Parisiis, 1901—.

S. Romanae Rotae Decisiones seu Sententiae, Vol. I-VI, Romae, 1912-1922.

S. Romanae Rotae Decisiones Nuperrimae, studio ac diligentia Belisarii Cristaldi Romani, 10 vol. (1684–1706), Romae, 1751–1763.

Syntagma Institutionum Novum, B. J. Polenaar, Lugduni Batavorum, 1876.

Theod. Cod. = *Theodosiani Libri XVI cum Constitutionibus Sirmondianis et Leges Novellae ad Theodosianum Pertinentes,* ed. P. Krueger, Th. Mommsen, P. M. Meyer, 3 vol., Berolini, 1905.

Thesaurus = *Thesaurus Resolutionum S. C. Concilii,* Vol. 128–167, Romae, 1869–1908.

II. AUCTORES

Aichner, S., *Compendium Iuris Ecclesiastici,* 2 ed., Brixiniae, 1905.

Alexander, J., *Commentaries on the Law of Wills,* 3 vol., San Francisco, 1917.

Amostazo, J., *De Causis Piis,* Lugduni, 1686.

Augustine, C., *A Commentary on the New Code of Canon Law,* 7 vol., St. Louis, 1920–1923.

———, *The Pastor According to the New Code,* St. Louis, 1923.

———, *The Canonical and Civil Status of Catholic Parishes in the United States,* St. Louis, 1926.

Ante-Nicene Fathers, American Reprint of Edinburgh Edition, 9 vol., 1899–1905.

Baart, P., *The Tenure of Catholic Church Property in the United States,* Marshall, Mich., 1900.

Badii, C., *Institutiones Iuris Canonici,* 2 vol., 3d ed., Florentiae, 1921.

Baldwin, J., *Modern Political Institutions,* Boston, 1898.

Ballerini, A.-Palmieri, D., *Opus Theologicum Morale,* Prati, 1892.

Bareille, A., *Oeuvres Completes de St. J. Chrysostome,* 17 vol., Paris, 1865.

Barbosa, A., *Iuris Ecclesiastici Universi,* Lugduni, 1660.

———, *Praxis Exigendi Pensiones,* Lugduni, 1663.

———, *Tractatus Varii,* Lugduni, 1660.

———, *Collectanea Doctorum in Ius Pontificium Universum, Lugduni,* 1666.

———, *De Officio et Potestate Episcopi,* Lugduni, 1656.

Bargilliat, M., *Praelectiones Iuris Canonici,* 2 vol., 37th ed., Parisiis, 1923.

Batiffol, P., *Primitive Catholicism,* London, 1911.

Bartlett, C. J., *The Tenure of Parochial Property in the United States,* Washington, 1926.

Baumgartner, R., *Conclusiones ex Quinque Libris Decretalium Deductae,* 2 vol., Romae, 1759.

Benedictus XIV, *De Synodo Dioecesana,* 2 vol., Venetiis, 1767.

Blat, A., *Commentarium Textus Codicis Iuris Canonici,* Liber III, *De Rebus,* Romae, 1923.

Bogardus, J., *A History of Social Thought,* Los Angeles, 1922.

Bondroit, A., *De Capacitate Possidendi Ecclesiae Aetate Merovingica,* Lovanii, 1900.

Bonfante, P., *Scritti Guiridici Varii,* 3 vol., Torino, 1916.
———, *Famiglia e Successione,* Torino, 1916.
———, *Istituzione di Diritto Romano,* 4 vol., 7 ed., Milano, 1921.
———, *Storia del Diritto Romano,* 3 vol., Milano, 1923.
Bouix, D., *Tractatus de Iudiciis Ecclesiasticis,* 2 vol., 2d ed., Parisiis, 1866.
Bouvier, J., *Law Dictionary,* 3 vol., 17th ed., Third Rev. by F. Rawle, St. Paul, 1914.
Brabandere, A., *Iuris Canonici et Iuris Civilis Compendium,* Brugis, 1866.
Bruns, A., *Fontes Iuris Romani Antiqui,* 6 ed., cura Th. Mommseni et O. Gradenwitz, Friburgi Brisgoviae, 1893.
Cappello, F., *Institutiones Iuris Publici Ecclesiasticae,* 2 vol., Augustae Taurinorum, 1907.
Cavagnis, F., *Institutiones Iuris Publici Ecclesiastici,* 3 vol., 4 ed., Romae, 1906.
Cavigioli, J., *De Censuris Latae Sententiae,* Taurini, 1918.
Cerato, P., *Censurae Vigentes Ipso Facto a Codice Iuris Canonici Excerptae,* 2 ed., Patavii, 1921.
Clark, W. L., *Handbook of the Law of Private Corporations,* 3 ed., St. Paul, 1916.
Cocchi, G., *Commentarium in Codicem Iuris Canonici,* 6 vol., Augustae Taurinorum, 1921.
Colquhoun, P., *Summary of Roman Civil Law,* 4 vol., London, 1851.
Coronata, M., *Ius Publicum Ecclesiasticum,* Taurini, 1924.
Craisson, D., *Manuale Iuris Canonici,* 4 vol., 7th ed., Parisiis, 1885.
Cuq, E., *Les Institutions Juridiques des Romains,* Paris, Vol I, 1891, Vol. II, 1902.
D'Annibale, J., *Summula Theologiae Moralis,* 3 vol., 3 ed., Romae, 1891.
De Angelis, P., *Praelectiones Iuris Canonici,* 2 vol., Romae, 1877.
De Fargna, F., *Commentaria in Singulos Canones de Iurispatronatu,* 4 vol., Romae, 1719.
DeLuca, J., *Theatrum Veritatis et Iustitiae,* 7 vol., Coloniae Agrippinae, 1706.
Denzinger, H.-Bannwart, C., *Enchiridion Symbolorum Definitonum et Declarationum,* 13 ed., Friburgi Brisgoviae, 1921.
Derugerio, J., *De Testamento Canonico,* Neapoli, 1711.
Desmond, H., *The Church and the Law,* Chicago, 1898.
Devoti, J., *Institutiones Canonicae,* 2 vol., 4 ed., Leodii, 1860.
Dillon, J., *Bequests for Masses,* Chicago, 1896.
Dictionnaire de Theologie Catholique, Vacant-Mangenot, Paris, 1903—.
Dictionnaire Apologetique de Foi Catholique, Paris, 1916—.
Dictionnaire de Droit Canonique, Villien-Mannin, Paris, 1924—.
Döllinger, J.-Oxenham, H., *The First Age of Christianity and the Church,* 4 ed., London, 1906.
Donnelli, J., *Commentarium de Iure Civili,* 11 vol., Norimbergae, 1825.
Duchesne, L., *Liber Pontificalis,* 2 vol., Parisiis, 1886.
———, *Histoire ancienne de l'eglise,* 2 vol., Paris, 1907.
Fabre, H., *De patrimoniis Romanae Ecclesiae usque ad Aetatem Carolinorum,* Insulae, 1892.
Fagnanus, P., *Commentaria in Libros* Decretalium, 4 vol., Venetiis, 1696.
Farinacius, P., *Repertorium de ultimis voluntatibus,* Lugduni, 1644.
Ferraris, F. L., *Bibliotheca prompta,* 8 vol., Parisiis, 1858.
Ferreres, J. B., *Institutiones Canonicae,* 2 vol., Barcinone, 1917.
Ferrini, C., *Manuale di Pandette,* 3 ed., Milano, 1917.

Forcellini, A., *Totius Latinitatis Lexicon,* 4 vol., Schneebergae-Lipsiae, 1831–1839.

Funk, H., *Doctrina Duodecim Apostolorum,* Tubingae, 1887.

Fulton, J., *Index Canonum,* 4 ed., New York, 1883.

Genicot, E.-Salsmans, J., *Theologiae Moralis Compendium,* 2 vol., 10 ed., Brusellis, 1922.

Gierke, O.-Maitland, W., *Political Theories of the Middle Ages,* Cambridge, 1900.

Gignac, J. N., *Compendium Iuris Canonici,* 2 vol., Quebeci, 1901.

Giraldus, U., *Expositio Iuris Pontificii,* 4 vol., Romae, 1830.

Girard, P. J., *Manuel elementaire de droit romain,* 6 ed., Paris, 1918.

Harduinus, J., *Acta Conciliorum et Epistolae Decretales ac Constitutiones Summorum Pontificium,* 12 vol., Parisiis, 1715.

Hergenröther, P.-Hollweck, J., *Lehrbuch des Katholischen Kirchenrechts,* Frieburg im Breisgau, 1905.

Highmore, H., *View of the History of Mortmain, London,* 1809.

Hunter, J., *Introduction to Roman Law,* London, 1908.

Jarman, T., *A Treatise on Wills,* 2 vol., 2d ed., Boston, 1893.

Kenrick, F., *Theologia Moralis,* Philadelphiae, 1842.

———, *The Primacy of the Apostolic See Vindicated,* 4 ed., Baltimore, 1855.

Krueger, H.-Brissaud, J., *Histoire des Sources du Droit Romain,* Paris, 1894.

LaCroix, L., *Theologia Moralis,* Paris, 1866.

Lanciani, J., *Pagan and Christian Rome,* Cambridge, 1893.

Laurentius, J., *Institutiones Iuris Ecclesiastici,* Friburgi Brisgoviae, 1908.

Laymann, P., *Theologia Moralis,* Venetiis, 1719.

Lega, M., *De Iudiciis Ecclesiasticis,* 2 vol., Romae, 1905.

Lehmkuhl, A., *Theologia Moralis,* 2 vol., Friburgi Brisgoviae, 1896.

Lingen, C.-Reuss, P. A., *Causae Selectae in S. Cong. Cardinalium Conc. Trident. Interpretum Propositae,* Ratisboniae, 1871.

Maine, H., *Ancient Law,* 3 ed., New York.

Mamachio D., *Origines et Antiquitates Christianae,* 6 vol., Romae, 1841.

Maroto, P., *Institutiones Iuris Canonici,* I, Matriti, 1918.

Marucchi, J., *Elements d'Archeologie Chretienne,* Paris, 1905.

Mazzella, H., *De Religione et Ecclesia,* Romae, 1885.

MPG = *Migne, Patrologia Graeca.*

MPL = *Migne, Patrologia Latina.*

Morey, J., *Outlines of Roman Law,* New York, 1891.

Moyle, H., *Imperatoris Iustiniani Institutiones,* 5 ed., Oxford, 1923.

Muirhead, J., *Historical Introduction to the Private Law of Rome,* Edinburgh, 1886.

Neyraguet, J., *Compendium Theologiae Moralis,* Turnaci, 1841.

Nicene and Post-Nicene Fathers (First Series), edited by P. Schaff, 14 vol., New York, 1898–1903.

Nicene and Post-Nicene Fathers (Second Series), edited by P. Schaff and H. Wace, 14 vol., New York, 1900–1904.

Noldin, H., *Summa Theologiae Moralis,* 3 vol., 25 ed., Oeniponte, 1922.

Pacchioni, J., *Corso di Diritto Romano,* 3 vol., Torino, 1920.

Pallottini, S., *Collectio Omnium Conclusionum et Resolutionum.......S. C. Concilii,* 17 vol., Romae, 1868–1893.

Palmieri, H., *Tractatus de Romano Pontifice,* Romae, 1891.

Paquet, L. A., *Droit Public de l'Eglise,* 2 ed., Quebec, 1916.

Phillips, H., *Compendium Iuris Ecclesiastici,* Ratisboniae, 1875.

Pollock, F.-Maitland, F. W., *History of English Law before the Time of Edward I*, 2 vols., Cambridge, 1895.
Pruemmer, D., *Manuale Iuris Canonici*, 3 ed., Friburgi Brisgoviae, 1922.
Rätzinger, P., *Geschichte der kirchenlichen Armenpflege*, Freiburg im Breisgau, 1884.
Rawlinson, J., *Notes on the Mortmain Acts*, London, 1877.
RCL = *Ruling Case Law*, edited by W. M. McKinney and B. A. Rich, 28 vol., 1914–1921; Supplement, 5 vol., 1921–1925.
Reiffenstuel, A., *Ius Canonicum Universum*, 7 vol., Parisiis, 1864–1870.
Redoano, G., *Tractatus de Alienationibus Rerum Ecclesiarum*, Placentiae, 1589.
Retzbach, J., *Die Verbindlichkeit formloser letzwilliger Verfügungen zu frommen Zwecken noch dem alten und neuen Kirchenrecht*, Freiburg im Breisgau, 1917.
Richter = *Canones et Decreta Conc. Tridentini—edidit A. L. Richter*, Lipsiae, 1853.
Rivet, L., *Institutiones Iuris Ecclesiastici*, 2 vol., Romae, 1914.
Rood, J. R., *A Treatise on the Law of Wills*, Chicago, 1904.
Roskovany, Aug. de, *Monumenta Catholica pro Independentia Potestatis Ecclesiasticae ab Imperio Civili*, 13 vol., Nitriae, 1847–1879.
Roper, R., *A Treatise on the Law of Legacies*, 2 vol., 4 ed., Philadelphia, 1848.
Rubei, L., *Resolutiones Practicabiles circa Testamenta aliaque Dispositiones ad Pias et non Pias Causas*, Lugduni, 1676.
Sägmüller, J., *Lehrbuch des Katholischen Kirchenrechts*, Friburgi Brisgoviae, 1904.
Sanguineti, S., *Iuris Ecclesiastici Institutiones*, Romae, 1890.
Santi, D., *Praelectiones Iuris Canonici*, Ratisbonae, 1886.
Savigny, S.-Scialoja, A., *Sistema del Diritto Romano Attuale*, 7 vol., Torino, 1888.
Savigny, S., *Traite de la Possession en Droit Romain*, 2 ed., Paris, 1870.
Scavini, P., *Theologiae Moralis Universae Compendium*, Parisiis, 1847.
Scheys, J., *De Iure Ecclesiae Acquirendi et Possidendi Bona Temporalia*, Lovanii, 1892.
Schmalzgrueber, F., *Ius Ecclesiasticum Universum*, 6 vol., Romae, 1844.
Schopf, *Handbuch des Katholischen Kirchenrechts*, 4 vol., Schaffhausen, 1858.
Schupfer, A., *Manuale de Storia del Diritto Italiano, Citta de Castello*, 1908.
Sebastianelli, G., *Praelectiones Iuris Canonici*, 2 vol., 2 ed., Romae, 1905.
Sherman, C. P., *Roman Law*, 3 vol., 2 ed., New Haven, 1922.
Shouler, J., *Law of Executors and Administrators of Wills*, 2 vols., 5 ed., Albany, 1915.
Smith, S., *Elements of Ecclesiastical Law*, 3 vol., New York, 1883.
———, *Compendium Iuris Canonici*, 4 ed., Neo Eboraci, 1890.
Sohm, R., *Kirchenrecht*, Muenchen und Leipzig, 1926.
Solieri, F., *Institutiones Iuris Ecclesiastici*, 2 ed., Romae, 1921.
Solmi, G., *Storia del Diritto Italiano*, Milano, 1918.
Sporer, S., *Theologia Moralis*, Paderbornae, 1901.
Tarquini, C., *Iuris Ecclesiastici Publici Institutiones*, Romae, 1887.
Taunton, E., *The Law and the Church*, London, 1906.
Tiffany, C., *Real Property*, 2 vol., Chicago, 1912.
Thomassinus, L., *Vetus et Nova Disciplina Ecclesiae circa Beneficia et Beneficiarios*, Venetiis, 1773.

Tonduti, C., *Tractatus de Pensionibus Ecclesiasticis*, Lugduni, 1661.
Toso, A., *Ius Pontificium*, Romae, 1921—.
Uhlhorn, J., *Christian Charity in the Ancient Church*, New York, 1883.
Vermeersch, A., *Questiones de Iustitia*, 2 ed., Brugis, 1904.
Vermeersch, A.-Creusen, J., *Epitome Iuris Canonici*, 3 vols., 2 ed., Brugis, 1925.
———, *Summa Novis Iuris Canonici*, 2 ed., Brugis, 1918.
Viard, J., *Histoire di la Dime Ecclesiastique*, Dijon, 1909.
Viard, M., *La Didascalia des Apotres*, Langres, 1906.
Vidal, P., *Institutiones Iuris Romani*, Prati, 1917.
Vinogradoff, H., *Roman Law in Medieval Europe*, London, 1909.
Vogt, J., *Das kirchliche Vermögensrecht*, Cöln, 1910.
Waltzing, J. P., *Les Corporations Romains et la Charite*, Louvain, 1895.
Wernz, F. X., *Ius Decretalium*, 6 vol., Romae, 1908–1913.
Wex, J., *Manipulus Decimarum*, Oenipontei, 1692.
Winterstein, J., *Der Begriff de Kirche in kirchenlichen Vermögensrecht*, 2 vol., Leipzig, 1888.
Woerner, J., *American Law of Administration*, 2 ed., Boston, 1899.
Woywod, S., *A Practical Commentary of the Code of Canon Law*, 2 vol., New York, 1925.
Zallinger, J., *Institutiones Iuris Ecclesiastici*, 6 vol., Romae, 1832.
Zitelli, Z., *Apparatus Iuris Ecclesiastici*, 2 ed., Romae, 1888.
Zollman, C., *American Civil Church Law*, New York, 1917.
———, *American Law of Charities*, Milwaukee, 1924.

III. PERIODICA.

American Ecclesiastical Review, 75 vol., 1889–1926.
Analecta Ecclesiastica, Revue Romaine, F. Cadène, Vol. I-IV., Romae, 1893-1896.
Commentarium pro Religiosis, 7 vol., Romae, 1920–1926.
Ius Pontificium, ephemerides iuridica, auctore A. Toso, 6 vol., Romae, 1921–1926.
Periodica = *De Religiosis et Missionariis Supplementa et Monumenta Periodica*, 15 vol., Brugis, 1908–1925.

Universitas Catholica Americae

WASHINGTON, D. C.

FACULTAS IURIS CANONICI

1926–1927

No. 41

DEUS LUX MEA

THESES

QUAS

AD DOCTORATUS GRADUM

IN

IURE UTROQUE

APUD UNIVERSITATEM CATHOLICAM AMERICAE

CONSEQUENDUM
PUBLICE PROPUGNABIT

GULIELMUS J. DOHENY, C.S.C., A.B.

IURIS UTRIUSQUE LICENTIATUS

HORA IX A.M. DIE XXV MAII A.D. MCMXXVII

ROMAN LAW.

I. The Development of Roman Law.
II. The "Corpus Iuris Civilis" Considered as to Source and Content.
III. Historical and Juridical Importance of the Institutes of Gaius.
IV. Juridical Concept of the Roman Family.
V. Paternal Power (Patria Potestas).
VI. Adoption.
VII. Enslavement.
VIII. Manumission.
IX. Rights and Duties of "Coloni."
X. Legal Personality in Roman Law.
XI. Loss of Legal Status and Its Effects.
XII. Liberty.
XIII. Citizenship.
XIV. Corporations.
XV. Institutions
XVI. Mancipation.
XVII. Tutorship.
XVIII. Curatorship.
XIX. Bethrothment.
XX. Marriage.
XXI. Divorce.
XXII. Legitimation.
XXIII. Ownership.
XXIV. Prescription.
XXV. Last Wills.
XXVI. Legacies.
XXVII. Codicils.
XXVIII. Statute Actions.
XXIX. "Litis Contestatio."
XXX. Interdicts.

INTERNATIONAL LAW.

XXXI. Nature, Division and Scope of International Law.
XXXII. Sources of International Law.
XXXIII. Rights of Sovereign States.
XXXIV. Acquisition of Territorial Jurisdiction.
XXXV. Immunity.
XXXVI. Extradition.
XXXVII. Diplomacy and International Relations in Times of Peace.
XXXVIII. Treaties.
XXXIX. The Monroe Doctrine.
XL. International Law of Neutrality.

CANON LAW.

XLI.	Canones 1–7	De normis introductoriis.
XLII.	Canones 8–24	De legibus ecclesiasticis.
XLIII.	Canones 80–86	De dispensationibus.
XLIV.	Canones 90–95	De domicilio et quasi-domicilio.
XLV.	Canones 99–102	De personis moralibus.
XLVI.	Canones 111–117	De clericorum adscriptione alicui dioecesi.
XLVII.	Canones 118–123	De iuribus et priviligiis clericorum.
XLVIII.	Canones 124–144	De obligationibus clericorum.
XLIX.	Canones 145–195	De officiis ecclesiasticis.
L.	Canones 215–217	De clericis in specie.
LI.	Canones 230–241	De Sanctae Romanae Ecclesiae Cardinalibus.
LII.	Canones 246–257	De Sacris Congregationibus.
LIII.	Canones 423–428	De consultoribus dioecesanis.
LIV.	Canones 499–537	De religionum regimine.
LV.	Canones 542–571	De novitiatu.
LVI.	Canones 572–586	De professione religiosa.
LVII.	Canones 587–591	De ratione studiorum in religionibus clericalibus.
LVIII.	Canones 637–645	De egressu e religione.
LIX.	Canones 738–744	De ministro baptismi.
LX.	Canones 762–769	De patrinis.
LXI.	Canones 802–813	De sacerdote Missae sacrificium celebrante.
LXII.	Canones 820–823	De tempore et loco Missae celebrandae.
LXIII.	Canones 871–892	De ministro sacramenti poenitentiae.
LXIV.	Canones 1019–1034	De iis quae matrimonii celebrationi praemitti debent.
LXV.	Canones 1058–1066	De impedimentis impedientibus.
LXVI.	Canones 1081–1093	De consensu matrimoniali.
LXVII.	Canones 1110–1117	De matrimonii effectibus.
LXVIII.	Canones 1203–1242	De sepultura ecclesiastica.
LXIX.	Canones 1327–1351	De divini verbi praedicatione.
LXX.	Canones 1372–1383	De scholis.
LXXI.	Canones 1409–1488	De beneficiis ecclesiasticis.
LXXII.	Canones 1495–1498	De bonis ecclesiae temporalibus in genere.
LXXIII.	Canones 1499–1502	De bonis ecclesiasticis acquirendis.
LXXIV.	Canones 1503–1507	De tributis ecclesiasticis.
LXXV.	Canones 1508–1512	De praescriptione.
LXXVI.	Canones 1513–1517	De ultimis voluntatibus.
LXXVII.	Canones 1572–1593	De tribunali ordinario primae instantiae.
LXXVIII.	Canones 1598–1601	De Sacra Romana Rota.
LXXIX.	Canones 1608–1626	De officio iudicum et tribunalis ministrorum.
LXXX.	Canones 1646–1654	De actore et de reo convento.
LXXXI.	Canones 1711–1725	De citatione et denuntiatione actorum iudicilium.
LXXXII.	Canones 1747–1836	De probationibus.
LXXXIII.	Canones 1868–1877	De sententia.
LXXXIV.	Canones 1878–1901	De iuris remediis contra sententiam.

LXXXV.	Canones 1947–1953	De correptione delinquentis.
LXXXVI.	Canones 1960–1992	De causis matrimonialibus.
LXXXVII.	Canones 2147–2156	De modo procedendi in remotione parochorum inamovibilium.
LXXXVIII.	Canones 2157–2161	De modo procedendi in remotione parochorum amovibilium.
LXXXIX.	Canones 2186–2194	De modo procedendi in suspensione ex informata conscientia infligenda.
XC.	Canones 2195–2213	De delictis.
XCI.	Canones 2215–2219	De poenarum notione, speciebus, interpretatione atque applicatione.
XCII.	Canones 2241–2254	De censuris in genere.
XCIII.	Canones 2257–2267	De excommunicatione.
XCIV.	Canones 2291–2297	De poenis vindicativis communibus.
XCV.	Canones 2306–2313	De remediis poenalibus et poenitentiis.
XCVI.	Canones 2314–2319	De delictis contra fidem et unitatem Ecclesiae.
XCVII.	Canones 2343–2344	De delictis contra personas ecclesiasticas.
XCVIII.	Canones 2346–2349	De delictis contra res ecclesiasticas.
XCIX.	Canones 2350–2351	De delictis contra vitam.
C.	Canones 2313–2314	De abusu potestatis vel officii ecclesiasti.

Vidit Facultas Iuris Canonici:

PHILIPPUS BERNARDINI, S.T.D., J.U.D., Decanus.
LUDOVICUS H. MOTRY, S.T.D., J.C.D., a Secretis.
VALENTINUS T. SCHAAF, O.F.M., J.C.D.
FRANCISCUS LARDONE, S.T.D., J.U.D.
MANUEL DE OLIVEIRA LIMA, L.H.B.

Vidit Rector Universitatis:

✠Thomas J. Shahan, S.T.D., J.U.L., LL.D.

VITA.

William J. Doheny, C.S.C., was born May 30, 1898 in Merrill, Wisconsin, where he received his elementary education at St. Francis Parochial School.

He spent two years at St. Francis Seminary, Milwaukee, Wisconsin, and completed his preparatory and collegiate studies at St. Norbert's College, West Depere, Wisconsin, where he received the degree of Bachelor of Arts in 1919. He then entered the novitiate of the Congregation of Holy Cross at Notre Dame, Indiana. He began his theological studies at Holy Cross College, Brookland, D. C., in 1920 and was ordained to the priesthood in June, 1924, at Notre Dame.

He matriculated as a candidate for the degree of Doctor of Canon and Roman Law at the Catholic University of America in October, 1922. He followed supplementary courses in American Church History, Papal Diplomacy and International Law in addition to the regular course of studies prescribed in the School of Canon Law. In June, 1924, he received the degree of Licentiate in Canon Law and in 1926 was awarded the Licentiate in Roman and Canon Law.

www.ingramcontent.com/pod-product-compliance
Lightning Source LLC
LaVergne TN
LVHW050204080826
844660LV00012B/353

* 9 7 8 0 8 1 3 2 2 2 3 0 1 *